FOR THE RIDE

XXXXXXXXXXXXXXXXXXXXXXXXXXXXXXXXXXXXXXXXXXXXXXXXXXXXXXXX
XXXXXXXXXXXXXXXXXXXXXXXXXXXXXXXXXXXXXXXXXXXXXXXXXXXXXXXX
XXX   XXX

ALSO BY ALICE NOTLEY

165 Meeting House Lane 1971

Phoebe Light 1973

Incidentals in the Day World 1973

For Frank O'Hara's Birthday 1976

Alice Ordered Me to Be Made 1976

A Diamond Necklace 1977

Songs for the Unborn Second Baby 1979

Dr. Williams' Heiresses 1980

When I Was Alive 1980

How Spring Comes 1981

Waltzing Matilda 1981, reissued 2003

Tell Me Again 1982

Sorrento 1984

Margaret & Dusty 1985

Parts of a Wedding 1986

At Night the States 1988

From a Work in Progress 1988

Homer's Art 1990

The Scarlet Cabinet (with Douglas
Oliver) 1992

To Say You 1993

Selected Poems of Alice Notley 1993

Close to me & Closer . . . (The Language
of Heaven) and Désamère 1995

The Descent of Alette 1996

etruscan reader vii (with Wendy Mulford
and Brian Coffey) 1997

Mysteries of Small Houses 1998

Byzantine Parables 1998

Disobedience 2001

Iphigenia 2002

From the Beginning 2004

Coming After: Essays on Poetry 2005

City Of 2005

Alma, or The Dead Women 2006

Grave of Light: New and Selected
Poems 1970–2005 2006

In the Pines 2007

Above the Leaders 2008

Reason and Other Women 2010

Culture of One 2011

Songs and Stories of the Ghouls 2011

Secret I D 2013

Negativity's Kiss 2014

Manhattan Luck 2014

Benediction 2015

Certain Magical Acts 2016

Eurynome's Sandals 2019

XXXXXXXXXXXXXXXXXXXXXXXXXXXXXXXXXXXXXXXXXXXXXXXXXXXXXXXX
XXXXXXXXXXXXXXXXXXXXXXXXXXXXXXXXXXXXXXXXXXXXXXXXXXXXXXXX

FOR THE RIDE

ALICE NOTLEY

PENGUIN POETS

PENGUIN BOOKS

An imprint of Penguin Random House LLC
penguinrandomhouse.com

LIBRARY OF CONGRESS CATALOGING-IN-PUBLICATION DATA
Names: Notley, Alice, 1945– author.
Title: For the ride / Alice Notley.
Description: [New York] : Penguin Books, [2020] | Series: Penguin poets
Identifiers: LCCN 2019033280 (print) | LCCN 2019033281 (ebook)
| ISBN 9780143134572 (paperback) | ISBN 9780525506386 (ebook)
Subjects: LCSH: Dystopias—Poetry. | Science fiction poetry, American.
Classification: LCC PS3564.O79 F67 2020 (print)
| LCC PS3564.O79 (ebook)
| DDC 811/.54—dc23
LC record available at https://lccn.loc.gov/2019033280
LC ebook record available at https://lccn.loc.gov/2019033281

Printed in the United States of America
1 3 5 7 9 10 8 6 4 2

Set in Classic Grotesque Std
Designed by Sabrina Bowers

Acknowledgments

Three sections of *For the Ride* have previously been published in *Golden Handcuffs Review* (thank you, Lou Rowan) and one section in *Poetry Salzburg Review* (thank you, too).

To Anyone

Contents

Preface

There is a room of walls which come alive with images and words . . . like a mind? in a beginning that's first an ending—get it? You'll have to decipher what's going on, as it happens. Just like I did. I started out in the l'Orangerie in Paris with Monet's *Water Lilies*, and their pond, but then I, or someone, became One, on a journey to another dimension to save Words from their demise, if there were really an Apocalypse—I mean if there were and so *all* of language were lost. "Save the Words" is the title of chapter II. This poem goes pretty far, and terrifies me, but it should be read for pleasure. A story, with characters, and illustrations, and qualities of humor and tenderness. Note further that on the ark that takes off from the pond, the Survivors have with them an Anthology of poetry which is quoted from: only poems can deal in the inexplicable—what really goes on. And each of the poem's characters finally becomes poems— nothing else left to one. I mean I don't know exactly what happened; I might even have to tell this story again sometime. There are glyphs or paint or matter or spirit everywhere, it keeps changing before your eyes or whatever one has.

I

THE GLYPH OF CHAOS
WITH WILLOWS

Back up and reenter glyph again, one. Wasn't one always there?
Yes but not consciously. First capitalize the name, One. Okay,

What about beauty? Oh the glyph's beautiful, mysterious,
possibly damning in the sense one can't go back on it, One.

One sees chaos, glyph's own background, rippled cloudy but grainy—
gradations of blue from navy to pale, shimmery, irregular . . .
One, oh One, hear tenses fall. Clanks about One of Unseen.
One doesn't know what's happening here! One shouts at no one. Birds fly,
aren't appearing, shadows flutter in, out of the grain, not in time—

Oh but One's not in time, what's One in? Chaos, beautiful chaos—
But, too, One's in glyph and it's hard; learning a new way to go,
that is, talk? proceeding on through . . . oh this might be round, rounded.

There are transversals, blurry poles—no they are lines One can't think
talk correctamente ly. Mental. One can't leave here forever?

Lines hold it up, why? Collapse isn't logical either, One.
Who's speaking to One? says the One. The foundational voice, One's.

They are lines of words in some langue . . . Why can't One read what's within?
Oh but One can. That's why One's changing, having entered this star
neither civil nor unwelcoming in its peaceful disorder;
never proclaiming one color. One wanders letting blues fall
embuing One, embluing one, c'est jolie in here, pas laid—

doesn't make one afraid of it, identityless mixages
of the more colors now, cerise, rose, and peach, then matte dark.

Oh what do the lines say to One? or to any one of the ones
sealed as ones are; senses are seals, unifying, at one's wish,
the one into one like those; could see a lot more being *here*?

The voice says, When one enters here, the seals come off gradually.
For this is one's parent chaos, timeless, shimmering, the old.

One seems not supposed to think, in what langue? One's head's opaque, alive—
opaque's alive, is One? How does One know that One's alive, conscious?
Stupid words, from any old language. Tints swirl in the word head;
One was born to be another's creature, what is One doing here

in the first thought surrounded by word parts without a form, only
ripples of pigment ghosts? One likes the sudden shadow of greened black
containing a non-rose, red fist, mouth swell. One's former other one,

mate or is it silky seal, gets up naked, from a bed to show—
in One's imaging head—sheet of words with some replaced, edited,
meaning ignorance censoring ignorance. Seals can't know much . . .
now One knows less, that's good. Lost in glints, on the walls of the glyph—

walls? Ain't walls or a thing. Should stay or go? Can't go to the bathroom here,
senses have been cleaned out. Don't have organs, aren't in this new percept.
Cascade of white pink strokes. Trying to read. It's just color, o dope.

One had to go to a bed by oneself. One became one's own seal
past tense, isn't it gone? Falls again, clunk. What tense is One in now?
One has the name of only personal pronoun here, in the tense too that's one,
letting it all fall to pieces of aught. One's so sick of the seals,
their feelings and their deaths. Now One has died, more or less, and that's cool?—
tree hair blaze of a naught—is it something? Now let go of One's words—
copper ripples in dark. Muffle, rien? Psst, croo-oo, ping, ba bah.

Then One's sounds in torrent. As the binging proliferates One freaks . . .
Jump up and down, timing. No one's around; there's no time if unwatched.

Fa-ti-gué. Think in thoughts. Oh more like clots. Lovey dovey of isles,
One wants to do it oneself—one makes the glyph, doesn't one? It's tonal
not allegorical. Coping agent, laminate One's rout, bout . . .

the coping agent's dissolved. What if it's hell? Just read it, stupid.

Ahem. Invite extinct obscura in. Quelle porte of this here glyph?
One used to say I and you, they and self. There was a shard-woman . . .
Go to pieces, one fool. One are the lost. Right in the breezy loss.
One likes it hereabouts, no arguments, puny thoughts like blippings;

chirp dream of lookalikes, chimes without verb. One drops a laugh, it's weird.

Open mouth: squawk and then *Li-sez*. One wants to read some word strings.
But one don't speaking right. Didn't or can't plafond of les nuages.
There was man in the store: what is a man? Goes to pieces. The door—

no one could find the door. Unless one's damaged or almost dead . . .
Leave that for just a while. It is essential to gibber, wisely—
this is One's coma, like. Man sold rational parts like marks on page.
Marks on page signify animal sounds. *These* marks came before sounds . . .

Prove it, One. Only One's here: One makes the truth. One says what was the first:
Nothing no verb tenses, get it? A one in a coma finds out . . . matter *is* marks

reading strings of willowlike entwinings on the blue coma walls,
where the parts've fallen off of speech and time. Stand by the emeralds.
One finds one, other one. That's one of the strands. *One is a native one.*

Tell one. The twigs writhing, les branches of parts. Gaskets and piston rings;

one is not, ones are not, separated. But only One is here.
One is composed of words like one makes in beginning, chaotically.
One makes them? One is making them, conscious. One knows it here, not chains,
posh garlands. Why? Why's not valid here. Making oneself now, oh One.

One is made, already! Precisely, but is making one also—
prior, not even born. One's reading, therefore, what's written by who:
had painted a lovely clasp singing in the head. The voice knows all.
One wonders if one wants structure? Later, comes after the—get rid

of history. It keeps the ones from coming to the quickly door.
Quickly all's changèd. One is another. It only took light years.

Read lines, thick intertwined. Tree trunks, what's that? Holding up sky. No sky.

One now know but nothing. Starting place already contains something.
Language of amoeba: In divisio, one thinks in all parts,
that is speaks, since the parts of one self understand each other.
One's body doth know one. Holding up sky? Looking for some food.
There's no food, at begins. No food in coma! Is this a coma?
Who knows? Who knows a thing? Not a damn thing. Yer accent's screwy.

Shimmery rose on cerulean ripples: but it's nothing. Figment.

Create scene. One shaking one, tells that one, You're too shut off!—Where
does this come from?—Shaken one's small, eyes wideset; has son.
Shaken one defends self wordfully, words the only weapon,
wideset eyes too, and frailness of the canny. What is this "shut off"?
Shaking here in the glyph. Any scene can seize one, slippage of
the stippled frescoes, pert creation. Choose what one wish, One.

First One is the shaker; then the shaken: all wits and projection.
But One wants to be One! Withhold oneself, Join not the combustion,
the communitarian fever to be ruled, set, open. One
wants to be shut off; One's eyes aren't wideset; One is not even formed,
no eyes—not One. Nothing real to see yet. A one wants to shake one,
as if somewhere in glyph thou art gone wrong, repellent but to whom.

One isn't necessarily any of those ones, any ones at all.
Amoeba hesitates to speak. You have to split to speak. One speaks,
One's ever spoken, even in glyph. Name of language is glyphese . . .

Thus someone's shaken One, or One shakes One; or One watches—which is
to speak. To write? One's body's written in the glyph. For who to read?

For who to? Lovely tongue saying nothing. No brain in amoebese—
oh what's a brain, One? Only the glyph is. Speaking glyphese, glibly.

One's been robbed of personhood; sorry, that's what it's like when one dies.

New scene wall-wise, from where? The present when. Who to who? Hands them.
Here are the parts, in black and white. They are the same as new words.
Neutral, forward, reverse. Great shift. One speaks in the neutral tense?
Clock on the wall: is unnumbered: one doesn't tell time here.
Frozen wall, arched openings to back of the store, of the wall—
it's not a wall, it's an image. One unwraps rounded part, obscure . . .
one standing behind counter, hands it to parts receiver . . .

this is what one has instead of manhood or other hood now—
does one really mind? not in comatose mental state, baby.

Lots of wrenches there on that wall. Screwdrivers, drills, hammers—
US Mer. Sea's full of the wall. Take these parts and speak newly.
Colored pond, lilies reappear. It's just a mind on One's head's
walls. But whose? Whose mind is this? One's? Who is One, One is asking

in the neutral tense; reverse won't go. Forward, forward won't either. No
future? One wants to make sense of fate. Fateless let go; wall shifting . . .

Wideset eyes defending oneself being shaken by that one still:
One isn't shut off from one! Loves the one but can't tutoyer one now.
One doesn't know how to speak, in the changing glyph birth into light.
One has a child, is oneself. Don't you one me, love. I've seen you naked . . .

One doesn't want to be yours, wideset eyes says to one in a blank room.
It's so blank here could scream. Don't want to be blank with the one here,
blank as love in the world renders ones with breasts so frail and so empty.
But *I'm* frail with my need, the one without breasts says hurting one . . .

Get out of that world. One must enter the glyph of the real . . .
Don't you leave me! the one shouts. The one can't if the one keeps hold like that.

The One, the original, watching this scene on the wall can't abide
it, Let One help. No, One can't. Ones in the wall are in the wall.
One without breasts is too strong. But why do the ones act so apart?
As if one's strength makes the real. Or one's wideset eyes. That's so stupid.

One watches pronounless til scene expires: it will come round again.
Doesn't everything, One? What if one said I for a brief moment?
I am yours, how horrible. One is one's—ambiguous. One can't
go back, what will one do? Without the comfort of the old pronouns . . .
Watch the walls. What tense is one in here? Who adjusted the tenses
in the world, all those years? Oh but One did, wading the tide of it—
it what? What it all is, it is all one, timeless and without sex.
I hate this! but the One doesn't hate it. One is interested . . .

Warm air and the black trees. Language eclipsed when One's head goes outside—
Oh but One's head is the glyph of the glyph. "Of" doesn't mean "of" now—

it's one selling parts again: Next to the Neutral Forward Reverse sign,
unreadable A Merchant Plea other side. One with special insight

knows of the teletype machine in the black. Always something in the back.

Glyph Central here, this space. Help One to stay right in Neutral, Present.
Light to right where there's none. One will now buy—it's a special adverb—
One loves one pastly, get it? In the glyph tenses dissolve rightly.
Haply One is pastly meeting the one that affects One the most.
That is One's air conditioning, One trows? One is supposed to love.
Hand One also the part callèd amour. No. The cliché closes.

Love is pastly is it? Or is it that love's not a part of speech?
Conditions aren't clear. Pastly or now? Never is One love-clear.
In dark swirl, fake motion—all motion fake?—couples of ones take sex
automatiquement, or is it with knowledge, prescience, adverbs?
Futurely One is born. That isn't it. One does it presently,
lilies pink of the void caress one's ocularity, pleasant—
pleasance and de la joie. Presently *then*. One's appropriate *then*.
One can never be so again in trees? Willows of backwards words
tuggingly, green-blue—black. Who is the heart? Qui is the shaman now,

Qui appears in futures invested lost and now. Qui is the shaman's part.
Who can one be comingly, who else but? Shaman of linguistic

sounds in time to keep time away from here. Never pictured, it's One.
Who is the shaman? Qui. It's One's other pronoun, the conjectural.

When—conjectural—One goes into depths of a wall, in One's mind's
eye, then where does one go? And who's there? Qui is the One who is there.

Qui the shaman is talking now: One is not materially
bound, if One thinks right, right into wall, where the language comes from—
Some of the words are bright yellow, bursting back, fixed against One.
Qui is living in the darkness, off to the side of the light.
Doesn't light differ from what's seen? If One's looking correctly
light peels away from the reflections. But the yellow is yellow,
to the eyes of One, who here has none, in the glyph of colors—
One doesn't mean colors at all, though One wants them meaninglessly

out of pastly habit to fix themselves as named as they seem.

One, says Qui, must make new language here. Why? Because someone in the dark
part's saying One must for the world's beginning again, destroyed.
Ones here—these words—are already doing it. These words alive.

```
w a i        w    w    w    c       i        ttttx  w
iw w a        w    w    w    h       n        rrrrx  i
l w w a       w    i    w    a       t        ooox  l
l wi  u       w    l    i    g       o        nnnx  l
o i i  x      i    l    i    r       t        cccx  o
wi  i  x      i    o    l    i       h              w
 si l  x      l    w    l    n       e        d'd'd
w ll s        l    r    l    o       d        aaax  w
i l o a       l    u    l    f       a        rrrrx  i
ll o a        o    e    l    t       r        bbbx  l
ll o a        o    r    h    k       rrrrx  l
o lw a        w    d    u    e       p        eeex  o
wo w a        w    e    w    o              w
ww l       s    s    d    i       n        ttttx
ww l            e    l    d        rrrrx  w
ww l       s    s    l    m       ooo    i
i  se          a    s    o       o        nnn    l
 l e           u    a    w       u        cccx  l
  e    d       l    u    s       t              o
  s    a       e    l    l       h        ttttx  w
  s       rk    s    e                  rrrrx
  o    p on        s                    ooo
          d                             nnn


     d  a rk            p a rt            cccx
pon    p                                m o u
     d   o  ét         po  p  nd          w  t e r
       nd      an      nd  o              a
          g
```

CHAGRIN OF THE WILLOWS

II

SAVE THE WORDS

A Lyric of One

Oh object, come to one's heart existing
again. One wants to like a thing or one
as in the past: oh one doesn't like, now.
One is differently gathered about one's
core—a tiny one, in the mind's eye of one.

The ones call out of small frogs' throats
to each other in the black brown pond,
the copper swirled pond where the light's
within . . . within one? within the wall
of sight? Within the connection between ones?

Here's what happens urgent in an Asian hotel, see glyph wall—

Asian one breasted must die for others. Doesn't make sense already—
Have to tell it, the one's named France. Stab her for the good of others,
immigrants like One. France is One? Doesn't know. Stabbed. Carried out
blanketed, and retarded boy—who must be France's son—cries.
One now crying for, pastly ways one's language makes ones die—"for
good of other ones"—stabbed for language. Wouldn't one say? One wants
hidden in black wall to be Qui. Shamanistically, dead.
One is the dead one, immigrant. One is the dead one named France.
One's not even French, One's like dead! Foreign One's France, that's the dead.

One forgot to say One is once an immigrant, pastly, or is One?

Sorry, One's dead . . . That's the language in the wall of fake brain.
There's no real brain. There's no science. One is the dead so alive.

Shamanistically, the dead Qui, dark in the wall of all,
speaks from pond mouth black, thickening voice of the glyph, asserts:
One's amoeboid now in the dank, splits into more, per line—
Why? Per line so One's more complex, several stories go on,
as the willows writhe or the yellow scribbles aimlessly paint . . .
Try to decipher more than one. Some pains for France's murder
seize One's pastly heart—isn't it there? Heart or France, or the One?

Doze between amber wake-up calls, parts store's calling, more business.
Need ones to buy more coma gears: Neutral one, two, or three, more—
slow or faster neutrals present. One wants to get to where One is,
don't the lilies spinning cry for theft? Any words to get there.

One's up as all night—there's no night—One mixes with other ones—
dream or story, pains in the ass. Oh an academy,
subterfuged matter, loves the One. It's a lurching of one
bodily towards. What's that *anatomy*, shamanistically
mouth's obliterating monad goes into third or fourth gear of
neutral, blocks lurchers out of way: One's here to stay in coma.
Can't organize into classes; kingdoms, phyla, or dinner . . .

One reels bodily at One to suck talent out of One's mouth,
mouth kisses, yellow of deceit. But Glyphese is One's lover!
Qui in the mouth, Qui is One's mouth, before the one can suck soul
shouts, Go back into the pond scum! Too formed for chaos! Backs off
but stays near other greedy one, with breasts, that wants One's soul too.

Parts store calls up, One needs more parts. One knows but's at static war,
that's the problem with neutral gear. One can't get away from ones

except via Qui, slipping soul into some pocketed words:
Qui takes One back to where One is. Can't explain anything. Is.
Want to explain. *Amoeboid, has to split off to know thing.*

One asks what's just happening. One demands presently visual clarity.
Why. One, because the One, was being taken advantage of—
The One was? But when amoeba splits, One is still the others, remember?
Yes, the others are poets, primal category, some ones like oneself,
trying to read primal glyph. But One's rather *in* the primal glyph.

Yes, dear, the two want power in the glyph. Already? Not ready. Recap:

One without breasts and one with. With desires Without who's empowered
in some other wall cliché or pond configuration, chaos's toy.
Without wants One because One's the best *poet* of the three of them,
more soul to suck? Is original amoeba; opened glyph door.
Without gropes towards One spurning With. Without feels entitled to One.
No one's entitled to One. Awakens sweating. To cool off in the pond . . .

One wants to stop all that from happening. Already happening,
Qui. One means that One's Qui, now in wall vert, suddenly green and deep,
drown, un peu, in the cool. Sheltered from breath, One dies
further; floats in parts of. Let some one down. Does One let some one down?
Would thing happen, arrive without the words? "Wideset eyes won't love one
enough"—ee-nough, love. Strip the sound *off*, floats away green and stark—
What's left then? the ones stop moving at all. Language not abstract, dear—

Shaman Qui screams a word: Blah! And Qui laughs. Words fluid of motion—

Wideset eyes now running from the Shaker. Shaker tries to catch up,
Run, One, run. Qui says, This is one definition of the verb "nude"—
one has nothing on but motion away. Wideset shouts One is not
gonna put up with one's anger wind! Cough of raining lover . . .

Qui says so. Meaning Qui is speaking Wideset's verbiage.
Wideset just an image: without one to see one one is dead?

Safe in oligarchy of the prior. Qui says one can escape.
Who says it? Or one can't? These beauty lines, willowed, will hurt the mind
running into the mouth of the next wall. Qui shouts, Next image please.
Can't tell the difference between words and anything that one sees . . .
Let ones see. Have to run! Shamanic mouth screams, Ones need more in . . .
Inflection. Describe the shaman's gender. Qui has none not at all.

Qui shouts, Auto parts store, sell me some cams, sparklets in one's headlets:
One's headlet needs a new term of address . . . Just have one in stock.

One runs from one, that is, Wideset's trying to be one's own oneness.
Shaman Qui is the voice: Who else could be? Run, Wideset, run and go,

Get an unlisted phone, fun on the steep. Earrings go bleep, of care,
down in underworld, nearly or was it underglyph, newed, wild

One has no home, is glad. Just the glyph One's hiding in, like for now.
Wideset hides in a green swirl on the pond. Not breathing. That one's safe.

Some one in this consciousness is in Underglyph; not Wideset but One . . .
under the pond that's not wet, one can't drown there, one finds fishy words . . .

under one, under one sings a black floating one, like a black cheese skin o lank,

another similar floating skin hanky cries, Not to talk about it!
About what? the One says floating likewise all splayed, safe in silly posture,
safe in something. Words crowd round, big old rags, skin rags ones are cut out
different shades of beige, black, brown, or just muddy. In the Underword, chill.

Ones need a you, shy you, do the ones here mingle? What about the "we" shit?

Forget it, relax, ones are cut off from the bod, pieces of what's called whole—

One's just the skin of a word. Where're the innards? Pretending to be smart,
up in the no-air air. Does one want verb tenses? Shredded, one was a tense,
says a tense all flopped out. One was another part, says one—who can remember?
Are ones known as anything but words here in wet? Does one have a story?
Ones never wanted to be anything but wet. One remembers, *the wet*.

Someone tried to kill one? floppy killing floppy neath the dark pond.
Ones here don't know which one does anything, thus or as to a why,
one now becomes what one can become: hanky becomes body shape like a trick—
Oh now one's a *word*, real category, bless one's hat or teeth!

Collapses. What's the point? One wants nothing. *The* One feels quite relaxed.
This skin's so undermined. One's just a hack, standing up pretending
to be meaningful. Nothing can happen. Who wants a structure—God?
I am God, says some skin. Word collapses. The word God collapses.
Who cares. Ones going further, says the One. Diving down, in element.

Is One looking for one? One's looking for language, don't know why.
Why don't know? One told to invent new language. By? A figment.

Bon. Ones are some figments. Invent this one! says a shapeless cloudy
stain in the non-water. Please invent one. What could this one be then?
One wants to be the word Love. Already have it. One wants to mean, New Love.

Take under advisement. Substantives aren't substantial here at all.

Just some part of one helping one get by, molecules, follicles.
Ones here are so flaccid, don't fall in love. Love's about falling in.
Does one want to fall in, in the new langue? *No* says the One, one wants
to be languid, not breathe even. One wants *more*, says the word-to-be.
For fuck's sake why, says One. One has had it. Potential words murmur,

What is *it*? One wants *reality*. And what's that? One already is, says One,
that seems enough to One. Ones want to be words, singing heads of light.
It's just so intensely back to what was. Past tense. Haven't had it!
One's always here. But a one's renewable as almost from scratch . . .

One remembers too much: love has killed One. What tense is that? Past love,
that's a tense. When one enters into a rock one can't regulate,
it's too hard. Death exists to make it harder. They're just words, though, here.
The words-to-be crowd round. *Not separate!* That's the first thing to know.

Lyric from Nowhere

The death word or message swims in one's wild cells,
those that refuse to be docile, grave, giving in
to the system. Oh death wanted one to depart
for the night its other hand, conglomerate
of words cohering. Love loves or hates that.

One had always wanted to be in love how stupid.
Managing no more the stores of orderly auto parts,
words, what was one saying? A shambles of
different sized stones, melting in one's head.

More stuff's arranged in front, appears to One, under the non-water:

One's an ideogram for Life a one says. Isn't one special! says the One.
Everyone's an ideogram, it says. Pearhead, arms, and torse—
an old ankh. Oh, says One, this is so dumb. One's going to zap One,
says the ankh sign, changing One's thoughts into some Egyptian ones.

Behold, One's eyes. Eyes are now two buzzards. See with vulture-shaped eyes.
One's composed of bird shapes in the sight place, looking at stylized pics,
underwater reflets. Hieroglyphs for the procession of things.

Well why not? What has One ever seen with one's handmedown op
optical process? But. Don't want that one to present One with real . . .
It's so cool, pleads the ankh. Flowering plant, feathers, half-disc, girl:
Chanteuse! Please says the One, don't want it—fussy. Says the ankh pleading,
Parade of lovely signs. Owls, barley, asps. The world seen in first words—

Dissolve this. Servant of a sovereign. One is going beyond:

One's more ancient than any of this. Older than signs, than tense for old.
Older than the new love? That's when old stops, back when the first
ones stuck together, or before One could talk? One could always talk,
even if not doing it as yet. Tenses. Hate them, rules of syntax—
Can't figure out how to say anything but talking in one's head,
see the shapes sticking together like love, fucking sentences.

Vultures fly, land and stick to the desert. Stars look like the word stars,
really do, ones really do, and sparkle is better as its word.

Thus be story of world, what else can one live out on page or real?
Returning to chaos, the first sender. Reemphasize and change.
Meander, as One does, meandering Egypt is all profiles,
clearcut thus. One is frontal, dissolving, falling into firstness,

swimming, swarming with words no one understands, partial p's and q's,
Masters of universe? One is that simply by being here now.

One is floundering, in Underglyph. One doesn't know, can't think straight
as of old when la langue was pure, when one said was, not like now—
it's all now with pronouns in space, lost and no quotidian.
Pretty chaotic. Just about ready to hear prophetic—
yet not future tensed—wordlets: Behold. Now is the time to save us!
It's that some voice, of words, says it! Words themselves want to be saved.
World is coming to an end means, Word is coming to an end.
In the global warming destruction of one's species as is known,
loss of language as one is the whole show. Build an ark of words.
One's supposed to be inventing *new* language, definitely
tearing down the old of gender, tensal submission, whatall,
pomposities to enslave one . . . Tear it down as ones save ones—
Ark of salvation and destruction of the old at same time.
Wake up! Tear it down! and save one. One is the species, words are.

III

RADIO FREE ARK

Who's speaking now? Qui is. Go back up to glyph walls to get started.
One's happy here, with limpnesses in Underglyph. One must save the words-O.
From other side of the words, on the side of the glimmer Qui doth command.
Save tissued words to be, and the words One chooses. How will One be able?
Still too flaccid from the Underglyph, One sputters. This of Chaos holds One,
anarchy of relaxation and doodling, in sounds of fibrous word shapes.
Here's when it starts. Says Qui. Says Qui, Origin's bottomless. Get up, One!

One's gonna build an old ark on the glyph walls and take some words to a shaky
point further on no one knows the tense of. Or it's now, already always.
Build the language destroying hierarchies of pastness, all too finished for
this crux, vortex of change that One is, and will die of, but the words can't.

What dies? Part of the tissue but not soul phloem. Or phlogiston. Save those!
Save those beautiful words. Okay, One now turns glyph to arkwise.

Floats One up; words to be must wait in Underglyph until callèd.
Doth One need a system? How can One choose? And can't build a dumb ark.
This for choice, proclaims Qui. Willow on glyph wall grows some branches
downward. They're messages, Qui says to One, speaks from dark of the pond—
where One was, but dark's big, stretching ever—includes every one's mind?
Pool of minds. One sees branches are long cloth ties, suggestions from the minds,
Qui says, of all the pooled. Mind wants an aspect of language to be,
sends message to the tree. So technical. Qui clears throat, wrack ahem:

One takes tie from wall, reads it calls up the comatose Parts one.
Parts one authenticates it. Or can get direct from teletype?
Let's have this process, uh, made formal. Ones'll build a new language—

sort of new—bricolage: why waste a thing? Always start with something.
Find out way to mix things for perfection's fear and its course. One will.

One will make a perfect thing; one will define perfect to suit one.
So it's not gist words, says the One. No it's parts of the whole langue!

One sees birds in the not-a-willow tree—vast arbre de ces chiffons—
these birds are large and green: dovelike parrots, perroquets escapèd
from ships to live in global warming metropoli, jolies mais
omineux. Always in future, a one. Don't need the tense, becomes

in present, in the now. One is acting under orders from Qui . . .
pond voice brain's the glyph. Mood of colors. Parts for previous
characters? Wideset, son, and Shaker to board eventually (faux
future—a possible tense) as three words. What about France and son?
France is dead. Not to One, or One is France. Is France a word? One's not.

One, oh what is the One? One is the frame. Ship to be built, and glyph.

One has terror of act. Time to begin. First rag selected's a tense: to begin.
Je commence with a new thing, really. Out of chaotic wall,
out of colors and transit meaningless, out of hung words to be,
rags hung down from projected shaman tree, one's forcèd to begin.

Here's how further it works: What One, One or Qui okays, is part,
or a word, goes on board. Where is the ship? Oh it's being built too,
north wall: but be careful what One say. Is there correct speaking?
Mais non, évidemment. Cette langue exists to help one change one's con-
ception of oneself. Yes? This new rag says: One wants expansive tense.

In the expansive tense, the present with adverbs detaches from
walls of glyph. Langorously not model but creeping spaciously
findingly permits cells, amoeboid of one, stretchingly to reach out
across glyph to real air. Is there real air? Just about. Air's its own,
not one's, but *the* common breath of ones; glyph doth include the real air?

yes, including vraiment the other air. Stretch to a better air.
The rag specifies this: Feel tense come into One with its own time.

Tense enters the One, like a drug, with some languor or danger—
dangerosité—One doth change. Words then of One, vice versa,
are infused as if time diminishes its hold, its stresses.
Parts one says into One's earring, Got it? Yeah, one has new glue . . .
But is this a coma really? Parts one: maybe *to be* is.
Wait! teletype's coming in. Says, At the beginning—not there,

no beginning, but at "it's an accident," unplanned something,
and it's part of the purpose, see: Where does that come from, purpose?

Oh, but nowhere. Like one's nowhere. Isn't that gist a question?

Qui says, One's somewhere, in the glyph! Only tense there is for One.

Is there a tense of becoming? Illusory, says Parts one—
one's coma's static in the store. Does One want this other part?—

A request for a provisional you. No. One can't accede . . .
can't provide a you. What does Qui think? Nightmare in the coma,

that's the glyph. Store's a sub station: keep the categories clear.
Why? Precisely. Say what One wants. Back in the reign of the seal
(provisional past) One is sealed. Remember, the one human body,
closed? Now One's bodiless of glyph . . . bodied but unsealed, indef-
inite, like infinite, undefined by the words of sealing,

"I am a man upon dry land." How dry that was, how bagged!

One needs you pastly to break seals. But they're broken forever—
if ones are all you, you's undone, as a form to make intimate.

Isn't there still you, as in heart? Seal's heart's wrapped in sealskin,
pastly, now heart's unwrapped by the expansive tense inclusion!
Where is the difference? In mind, it's in One's mind, different.
No one's like One. Who's talking all this time, Parts one or who?
Is Qul a confusing usage? Qui says, Not confused: Don't know
who's speaking. Is it Parts one who says, Ones all speaking together?

Another message from tree: Anthology needed to go on now—
Is "to go on now" a tense? One goes on now calling one's lover's name—
part of the expansive? Anyway, One's distracted, let's see, an Anthology—

message continues: Of what's being written, not so much of what was—
Why?—one discutes with rag—Need gems already in the new langue—
Not written, langue not known—Being written as langue is further known.
What is to be now is. What's to be is kerneled in each word that
comes out of the ones here or hereabouts. Ones aren't content with them

but they keep coming. Work with what is. Poems too piled neath tree

which will change into mast. How many sails? Variable like walls.
Where are the ones going? Purpose of ark is to weather without
knowing where it'll land. Maybe, the only sail is the whole tree.
What color is it painted. Shifting green, with a grey and blue—
partaking of ocean, ocean of change, and of novelty.

How soon does one depart? Pretty soon now. Ark's almost built. Callèd what?
Ark. Or maybe Radio Free something. Hey, Radio Free Ark?
One likes that. Look who's sneaking on board it: the two soul-sucking ones.
Does one really need them? They've vanished into the wood, One, like shades,
psychic haunts. Ones'll have to war with 'em. Inevitable it is.
Look! Parts store's being transferred to the hold. Oh but one'll miss pond,

oceanic now in a Storm. No more lovely Augusts with lilies and crushed
paint strokes dark like mind of One's own surface. Sometimes the Ark's crystal—

there! Glassy mass of ship, glinting against naval blue black passage.
Is this just a passage? Is it the rest? Is the rest a new tense?

One's language begins to lose clarity, or to gain, or One
abandons the concept. One expands and goes oh so suddenly—
Radio Free Ark pushes out to sea. Is it an ocean wide?
Or an image of that? Whatever it's, One's fearful, near wordless.

Who is pilot of this here ark? Qui is the ark's own pilot.
One loves Qui for it, so easy. But embarkment brings words
can't control. Waves of gibberish. How can One read a message
if One can't talk One's own lingo? Oh what is it? Won't abate
without règles, chaos's wavelets, sea of viscosity's hatrack,
head and tongue addlepated skull words, like an attempt-speak.

Keep next to dancers, flying fish. Seriously injured globe,
need One remind One of the truth? This dream is ending for ones—
Only accept it in opaque storm of the interviewed orb:

what language does Thou speak, oh world? Volontiers, volupté,
any ole balance, zézayant. One lisps trying to play the boneth,
xylaphoneth of niños, lizard babies, dinosaur-bone fashion.
Before, that was before this spot one's in, breaking down. To knees.
Save some words for someone who might survive on the dead fan flames.

Ones that send requests for the langue hardly talk a talk; mast tree's blown,

willow ropes whipping in vicious no-wind, crystal force mental danger.
Parts one calls up: Definite request for tense *to go on* through any:

present continuous with piquancy's staples: infinitive of verb
to continue, in to go on tense: conjugate: one goes on continuing,
ones go on continuing. Is that all? In this tempest that's just enough.

One's howls fly apart, One can think a little. Where doth go at time's end?
Time, the human concept, dies with the ones if the ones, all of them, do die.
Former the ones. Speaking to all the ones in One's mind of interlove.
What can the ones do to live? Is there anywhere to go on to, ô ones?

What, France, dies when everything one is appears to die, deformed?
One isn't *that one*, even if all the ones die together—
is one? Yes. Asian hotel room whipping around on the wall—
One's in wall, *is* wall, says Parts one, but realer than before. One needs—
what does One need besides a world, made of countries like dead self?
Dear of self planet's shrieking, stay back from One! to words I and we.

Ego walks vortex? I is destroyed—And who knows that? Qui does.

Can't live without world. Carry her body away, blanketed,
remember poppies, cornflowers, lark, and the troubadour's song
imitating flight? Oh be clear. Clarity's complex, not fact
singular; chaos doesn't destroy it, is it; angry now—

or, more active than usual. What else of One's language?

To stay alive one needs a tongue, more than ever. Parts one says:
Here's a little hit from the anthology. Keep one abounce.

From the Anthology

Leaving world for dissolution, must one save
personal carmen or amor, as for thou?
I have saved I for loving you, against one's
rationality,
I've saved I for you. It will sound foreign to
no-ears one's left with, as chaos takes us home—
What is us? The ones dissolving, Tyrrhenum

not really mare
overtaking ones on the way to time's town,
killing that for more than even saecula.
Older than Latin is the angry mother
whose marmor white sprays.
One can't speak but of collapsing sky and land
though longing for a personal structure
as defined by us, I save the I for you
just in case we're left.

One's mind's words going on going to pieces. La couleur jaune one's got,
ahoy, separating from anything, as if thou were thyself . . .
could be color like air? Not a, symbolical fraternity,
object cum sunshine or cowardice-ripped. Color's ripped free, is One?
Talk to me, Self, don't Say it. Qui is the One. One ripped off from some self—

Nothing to be lovèd. Unanchored One. Maritime is timeless,

putative of the brain. Thinking's not *it*, it never was, it's late.
There's another thinking—it thinks for you—From where? In space inside—
Where? Only imbeciles suppose that one's in one place at a time.

This here langue has to put one in more than one circumstance at a fois.

Second universe born. Okay? Constellations are different . . .
Going there with these shreds. One isn't shred. Bits of words on the tongue.
Bi o wo on th tng. Thusand yrahs. Mor. At one time yellow.

flag

p
a
s

d
e

p.   e   a
p.   little
p.   p   drapeau
y .   a
y .   s

y   .   l   t
y   .   s   l   t
l-------------------- e   é   l   t
l   e   h
l   e   l   i
l   e   n
l   s   wings of words   e
g   s   p
g   s   wings of words   a
g   e   ark   r
g   e   ttttssss
a_____e_____k
a supernimbus   k
a   surreally cognizant   bat-blue   thy self   careless   k
a   & its sister memento   qui   k
a   k
a   part   k
a   prepositions   k
a   part   ark or one   k
a   k
a   k
a   arrrrrrrrrrrrrrrrrrrrrrrrrrrrrrrrrrrrrrrrrrrrrrrrrrrrrrrrrrrrrrrrrrrrrrrrrrrrrrrrrrrrrrrrrrrrrrrk

IV

THE LANGUE CONTINUED

Previous universe. In a prior world there's another she.
Forbidden, tense and pronoun forbidden. Say one's in transition.
I watch her from a star. That's forbidden. Have to come from harsh star
as well as chaotic ark in order to change and save the word.

I'm in both places now. On the ark something's real and it's a smell.

Where does scent come from, One? It's more mysterious than color is—
Is it? No way to make it be abstract—stinks. There's a corpse somewhere.

Let's say ark's calmer now. Enough to smell something, some one says it—
Or was it something one once smelled somewhere? Pastly. Forbidden he smelled.
He? From days of gender. Smell lingers on, in the ark of saved words,
Radio Free Ark. How free? Woman's body, one says, but the smell

is unique, that of cannibalism. Ones ate One's body, hers.
Smell putrid also sweet, like none other. Hooked on eating her flesh.

Smell's still here. Permeates. Haven't they finished eating One? One shouts.

Ones can't finish, the smell's all over ark. Dark rue de Passé,
corpse in wall of one's fright. Face the odor. Which words are ones saving?
I can smell it from this star. As many worlds as one can be in
at one time, save these words. The rag says, Want to be in more than one.

Are they eating France's corpse? But it's One's, One says in hysterics.
The two soul-suckers smile. Can One understand what's happening, One?
Qui says, as One mouths, *They're eating One*, everything is of use;
but should it be? Should use be a dominant quality, a word?

They use me, I mean One. Inventing female as succor. Addicts.

Try to get this right this time. For the ones. Can't have her anymore,
she's One. The smell'll purge via storm, will come back again soon,
strike out will, no future. There's no future, if one's old enough.
Future's a way of killing One off. Of telling One to wait;
or that One's gonna die. I'm watching from the star. I'll never wait.

Getting rid of old verb tenses is a chore: don't wanna talk no more.
One collapses on deck. Sleep, baby; No. Tell One something newer.
Thine is the ark's corpse studded with wordlings. Not a corpse: skeleton—
it's a white bony ship, going nowhere, through the midnight stars now . . .
lull in the action; One's like a beetle, dark wings capelike around—

Can't describe consciousness, nasty technicians, 'cause it's all, too, they know.
Studded with the faint stars, it envelops. Constellation of egg,
there, shaped like origin. There's one shaped like words: *Becomes a kiss: why?*
One don't want to be kissed. One don't want to read someone else's mind,

up there. Erase those stars. Start over; don't spell. What is the ultimate
outside, Ma, in One's eyes? Illusion's richer than One thinks it is.
No. It ain't. Listening only to One, inside the beetle cape—
Before the slaves of their illusions come to make one join their forms—

Rest in these, Baby Cool. Aren't universes thoughtfully like thou?

Is One I or I One? Neither, all's One. Simultaneously,
above fray One's in, rests constellation of dark mementos, leaf-shaped,
not willow, generic: cutout feuilles. World One is never in
pastly—tugglingly calls. Never lived there. Never live there rather,
dratted past—history's tense—who can need it? Qui whispers, One doesn't,

these are constellations of the present: danger in shape of bee,
apis—swarming of stars. Starting again. Conflict on dead planet—

is it as dead as One? Yes One thinks so, in tense of going on.
Because there are other dead people, want to take over One?
That's it, even in death. They want to kill, words is it, or One's words,
steal or kill, still would kill One in the ark, want to order ark
into mirror of old leader on top, still, never let go,

dead power king of one, constellation being built—the old
creeps always back. Get up and kill them! Okay fearless etc.

Some ones are crying: opportune for some leaderly bullshit . . .
Climbs the mast or tree. But, says One, arising, who's here except words,
One, and Qui, and other phantomic amoeboid splits off One?
Qui says, the soul suckers aren't of one. The old bastard wants it,

Look! and both soul suckers are up there bouncing up and down in crow's nest . . .

There's no one to take over here! We want the words to be ours!—
There's no we here.— We say there is! We have a gun and a knife.—
If you kill Qui the ark won't go, Qui says, it's run by this Qui.—
We have our own Qui, the soul suckers say. Everything's our words,

we'll winnow yours away and take our choices into the future.

There's no future, One says, truly. Only this ark. Pull them down!
Soul suckers bounce on the ropes, the ancient pontific
charlatan and the breasted one. They still want One's soul, says Qui.
Take One's ark, change it to mush. Pull them down. They'll come back for One.

Shadow ghouls quickly escaping. One's got to work on words.
Qui says, Soul suckers can't let go. One, find the best of the words . . .
universes. What will be left of all? Words might just fly away

into void. Be lost. A few hunters and gatherers near mute . . .

Must save the way to mate with a face? Call it a one—not stamp it
though with old signs of fixity? The loved singularities;
eyes to pose as their past ones, only seeing a wall's fake spray,
beautiful as it is. If there's not much to see, eyes'll change,

if there's not much to say, One dies. Who though doesn't reflect light . . .

What light? says Qui. Or maybe nothing but light and heat?
Look! Shaker's stopped chasing Wideset. Exhausted, and ark's too tiny,
catching you there's nothing to do. Why're we here? says the male—
says, *I'm* saying what you call me. Collapses on grey deck paint.

Oh words be the guide now in the bleak tremulousness!

From the Anthology

Chaos grey calls, order is one's tongue or eye
is it? Can't order me though, ultimately
I'll say I, nothing matters to me
I'm only matter itself without bones

You put the bones in, your so precious pattern
It's all in your head, if you have a head there
It's just a delusionary tale, dear
make up your own language, my psychopath

Okay and one will. You can say I too, mean-
ing whatever speaks. Don't give a shit for she
or he, categories down in flood
demolished by the world's disappearance

Why are we still here? Chaos answers, I am
that's why. But not your linguistic subtleties
I want to be woman! says death—
Stop trying to regulate me, Chaos says

you're nothing but mass. It's too hot here, you say
It isn't a thing, hot or cold or loving
Make something out of it if you care
You're there, that's all there is to notice.

Here's another request from the tree-mast: What about weirdness of,
weirdness of saying one? There's no dignity one recognizes
to be gained in this usage. What about other pronouns as well:
they, it, we—what is one doing about? One's prone to babytalk . . .

Essentially correct, but who can care now? One says, Still one hears . . .
you? Big what about you? Problem is, can't care. Those words don't occur,
not anymore. That's what mutation's like. It'll keep growing now.

See what ones are saying. For example: Wideset says to kid:
Does one like those new stars there in the shape of a giant skate fish?
Kid says, One wants to get off this ark. Know there's nowhere to walk,
but if it's not water, maybe one can walk on it. Is one just
imaginary, Mom? Who knows? One doesn't know, or maybe does.

One says, Is one always imagined, or not until the world's end?
Then there was nowhere left to be but mind. Where does that come from?

Wideset says, Constellations mutate too: now it's a trapezoid . . .
Shaker says to the one, You're not my kid, I like you anyway—
Kid says, Why don't one talk like the ones? Why not say ones, like ones?
Shaker: I'm losing it . . . Because it's dumb. It's how it comes out now,
Wideset says. Intricate, making the same word mean each thing it can:

One loves *one*, on the ones' ark in the night that isn't old nature.
New stories must be told. Tell one one, kid says. There is a one who—
and is both one and who, in transpiring ark across the mind sprays
must beware the creatures flitting in the grain, wood of the ship's walls—

Are those *bad*?—Those ones want to eat the souls ones evince in their words.
Meaning what? Shaker snarls. Want to eat ones. Souls are words, souls are ones . . .

One's got a soul on one's tongue, says Shaker sarcastically. Little

guy. The ones, says Wideset, are equally nowhere in energy.
Mingling, without a hope; glad to be without madeup things like hope.

But old nightingales follow one, only in grey pretending . . .
Hear how birds out of one's mouth . . . aves ultimae noctis,
any sound. Ears go with noises. In another universe,
there aren't sounds maybe? Any logic so long as it mutates:

anything care of the feelers. No, the feelers might not work:
follow what one's saying? If one only talks to oneself,
don't need ears? Wideset's talking to One. Imaginary, says One.
Not imaginary! Wideset says. Parts one calls up from hold—

There's a pan-ark mutation on, nothing's making any sense.
Rag from the mast-tree asks for sense. Need for nonsense for a while,
One says, or at any rate can't stop. Who's in the undercooked moon?
Qui says, Who goes there? Others than Qui, at least the Qui that One knows.

Put the ark in neutral! One can't, Qui says, it's in the tree branch gear
scratching against the window of going to hell or senseless.

When One said I, there was love. Could change to O: O (one) loves you,
O loves U. One don't want to say it to one. Why not? One don't want to—

no, no O, I, U. One's choosing. For the whole thing? When One said
I love you, it felt like a lie. It was in code. But for what?

All in code. For what? There's no world, civilization's destroyed—
was the code for *it*? One thinks No. It was a chauvinist frameup,
France is dead in the frame of ark. Woman that was nothing real,

constructed for eye contact. I'll contact you along way
as I build monuments to me. Shaker nods, Reasonable.

One says, There's no you because one doesn't want to address you . . .
Ones talk to each other nonetheless. That constellation's a rose . . .

Just talking not addressing, in night of the changing placement.

All relationships be over, demands a rag, says Parts man.

Appears in bizarre sky, new sky of other universe arriving.

V

RETURN TO CHAOS

If one tells a tale, unending no-night, under those the new stars,
what tense will it take? Wideset's speaking. Something like memories come.
One walks down a river saying Bye Bye to a one who will die.
Is that a story? asks restless kid. Another kid joins ones, grave,
France's teenage one. Stories are futile, create new sense of time—
who wants time? says One. One walks down a river—
Wideset says—that's all. This time's contained within nondescript walking—

that one will walk away, and *this* one's gonna turn back, to go back.
Where? says France's son. Which one is one, Mom, says Wideset's son—Turns Back?

Of course, Wideset says. My mom can't turn back: France's son. Must die.
Maybe one can keep saying goodbye. Can one hold that part of it?

One's belt buckle's odd, Wideset replies. It's iron—on one who'll die—
It should be silver, shouldn't it, Mom? Kid says. The stone's yellow green;
disturbs one, says Wideset. One wants the other one to come *down* river.

Don't go! say the kids. One hugs the one. Then turns back from one, *up* river.
How long is the river? asks France's son. There's no length to it now.
Does it once have length? Pastly? Length depends on how far one travels;
it's not finite now. One, other one, walks up river. Now it's day.

Why? says France's son. One doesn't know; does it matter? When's day *here*?
Don't know. One walks up river towards no goal, just walking. It's pretty,
river's intricate, sandbars and trees. One sees a bird, a pink one.
There aren't pink birds there, usually, says Wideset's kid. How does one
know? asks Wideset. Don't know how one knows it. One is the same one as one,

maybe, a little. One likes the pink bird!: France's son. Very soft.

How far does one walk? Far as the bird. Bird'll fly away from there.
Maybe it won't go. One's still saying goodbye in night, belt buckle;
and one's still with pink bird poised to fly, in the daylight, both at once.
They are both one's friends: creepy iron belt buckle and the pink bird.

Pause. Ark's collecting heaps, transparent words, not only chosen words—
but what's said that's accepted without a fuss. Under the tree-mast piled
invisibilities almost glitter, near the elected slips,
rags, converted to use. Maybe the things, things that really count,
can't be seen, or in old parlance, be sold. Best thing about this ark's

no real commerce on it. Parts one calls up, One objects, got a store
in this here hold, one knows. How does one pay? Don't pay but one buys it,
pays with one's acceptance, of new usages and new attitudes,
dears. One loves this old store. Objects on wall, in mutational forms,
shine. Thine are one's fine wares: this is a noun, for chrissakes, séduisant,

gasketing, pistonal. One's coma's rock solid as far as basic
patterns, conglomerates. Changeable around some tenets of shape—

Chaos contains itself, it's something, one is too: no nothing is.
And one can't go to it. Coma: chaos: but not no thing at all.

One does want to go to, more like nothing. One can't be conscious of that . . .
But maybe could be something different from conscious. Say, asleep?
Asleep's another conscious, one thinks. Another one from that one . . .
conscious of nothing? Does one want the word "conscious" on the journey?

One sits on the deck. One is not conscious anymore, one's saying,
not as usual. Ones tend to project old patterns on the ones . . .
But, are now chaotic. Qui speaks here. Look at oneself. Matter spreads,
speeds up of the hands, they're in motion, there. Like on LSD, One.
Now. One is a point, in some mind still, one's one without one's old form,
but there's still . . . a mass. Being, its thought; always is that, isn't one?
Outside that locates one is vanished—one is *massive*; has forgot.

Could sing it into lovely pattern. Could create consciousness—
Poised, though, is serene. Informal, not being char-
acteristic. In any way. What does One do being that?

Ones lose it. No but *won't*, soul suckers blurt, will remain opposèd—
didn't mean to say that, *aren't* negative . . . Have reappeared in air,

like principles, or ghosts. One hardly recognizes them: can they
still take over the ark? Qui proclaims, *Changed*, let's see who these ones are.

One without breasts: One wants. What is there to want in *this* universe?
The only things are stars. Not even ones; though have brighter words here—
Have to have. One with breasts says, Each other. Need objects, objectives,
wails Without. Will have to invent some things, vent in circle rings—

can't control what is said, isn't correct. Define a new correct . . .

do want to control it. Oh unravel, says the One. One sees that
it's not quite time to start. Are before that, and maybe don't begin—
Can't ones just see how voices elaborate? Don't have to be what
one is pastly in life. Can't control it! shouts Without Breasts. Nor can
One, says One. Don't know who One is, One or one. Art thou entity?

Must exist, say the soul suckers, together ghast, what an idea, not—
Am speaking, are speaking: With Breasts, long blond hair, blond but as an image,
memory of hair. Everything an image, mutters One, and so might
One be. Thou or One, what matters it? The question's whose mind is this one?
It's an ultimate mind now, nothing here but ashy a prioris . . .

With Breasts is hysterical, Without's dumbstruck. Scared. Principles. One reflects,
emotions as principles of motivation. Supposed to be scarèd,
just some old shit. And now one's gonna cleanse the air, Qui says, with a blower,

will blow human hair everywhere one breathes, blow *you*, as you, the past *one*,
image of social, away! Watch out for the hair that cuts and wounds one!
Put on some masks! One wants to watch it, One says. Parts one's up with blower,
With Breasts' hair demolished. It shrieks, the hair itself, eeks small of disappearance . . .

Replaced by ghost hair, a corona of cloud wisps. Images always there,
Qui says. Is that existing? One's perceived, says With Breasts. Seen and can speak.

Shaker says, See and can talk, don't remember. One has changed, bien sûr,
words come from one not under one's control. Were they ever? One says.
If one knows who one is . . . Seeing without, eyes. Taught to see, just see . . .
It's all here, isn't it? In this chaos. All one was, unsorted:
nothing is ever lost. Don't say nothing! It's a meaningless word . . .

Is this a conversion experience? Shaker's intelligence—
but, in chaos, that's free of its bodies, one can assume It,

it's for having, one digs? One wants some smarts? Take 'em. Talk however.

Now France appears, for everything is here: Are a ghost? says her kid.
Am spirit that loved *us*. Can one explain it any more? Died *for*.

But there wasn't a for. Does one want word? For is a big old cheat.
Ones made one to die for, perhaps want revenge but can't remember
what ever happened. Parts disarrangèd, all mixed up in chaos;
made to know bit of one's or another's story. Dost thou want own?

Naked along highway . . . Don't want these words, don't want any shame now
not even another's, vicarious: story for borèd pimps.
Who was thine own pimp? President, or boss? Pimping soldiers, good kids?
Responsible femmes? Wait on Him, the overorganizer—
tell ones all what to do. France, femme, must die: *moi, I am moi, the one* . . .

Broke the factory wall bent against it by some one's willful hand.
In this new world will one have hands or will? Don't want anything,
dangerous, everything's dangerous except for the smaller words:
oh don't know what they are. Glad not to find. Story that's so painful,

tout mélangé dans la brume. One killed me. Who? All parts are in ones,
of some crime. Is it sharp? Is sharpness here? Is something abolished?

Maybe, says One, maybe. Or transmogrified. If the smallest ones,
if atoms can be reconstituted. Oh, can they be, but who—
Qui—can one ask except Qui, within one? Free ones from the statues.

From the Anthology

One would have loved thee, if Eros had insight
red, insolence or made an entrance. E didn't exist
all molecules of that thought scattered in l'Allée des Morts.
Who goes there? Qui covered in rubies, "my" blood.
A Life. What did one "shed," across the religious
miles, the concepts fought for out of mainstream ambition—
Where did *that* come from? Accepted and bright.

One's skeleton clanks but it can't talk, only the
"over meat" parts. Others won a prize before

the world, wafted across the paradigm of space,
ended: not that it exploded it refused—oh
ones—finally to conform to the prevalent
celebration of What's in My Pants. (Oh

blinds all around window oh blessed bonds
oh stamps oh signatures oh ideas . . .)

The idea of human love destroyed while one
was riding high. To get to the top, of the cadence,
one must be more purposeful than. Than than.
Extreme Happens: Eyes in the distance not there.

One whispers, Now il faut. How does one know? That word. Who knows a thing?
Useless words, but let's consider the words. Let ones. For One's embarked
into seas of verbiage to be repatterned, reconnected, Dear.
Who is Dear? Formerly you? of the breeze. What difference of things?
There's a little alleyway back of night. Or does it push right through?
Strewn with, or maybe not. Nothing correct. One's doodling, not to start.

Start. City of the words! But ones're still on ark—It doesn't matter—
Also still en été in pond. Also coma'd, dead, whatever.
Why start? Why ever start? On the ark's deck, or in the alleyway.
Beneath the chaotic stars or as star, to be One with it,

the Making. Dismantling and making. Ones have ever done so,
not always as *humans*, have had no nomenclature, betimes,
nor earthliness per se. Finity's a recent concept, human—
who cares about it now? One finds another position or scheme.

Word Tree

at
no
love   exile
from   the former
paves. . . . .   "forehead alley"
where carnage mental rubied the tongue
l'arbre du corps, hurt by grouped thoughts
that corruption. One only lived you'd say
there by assenting punish
but this is the future, dead.
        none ever lived here
          none built this place
      perfect for "thing" purpose
        these words hang from one emptily
polemic of   A
salt that's fertile   An
underrose arguer
        come live
         here
        activate
         the
        fabric

VI

DISEMBARKMENT
AT LOST CITY

One's found the lost city no one was ever in
made of words One's selecting, city extends from the Ark, as it goes
     along road of the dead, ragged
unforeseen being one is
                    always past or is, angelic idyllic
                    find it in some words, there is nothing else left
                    everything ended, one watches fall
                    human systems, not more humans but words
                    escaping with One into Chaos, mixage
                    And One gets mixed right into the caldron
                    or is it more like a chameleon
                    rumpled and least

nothing is most, here come words
those One loved or used with a wrist no wrist here, how come words are?
     because One is How Because mind's what there is over all in out
     prove it. what one knows, all science, is from In
          from knowing with a mind, who else's
                         One's the ancient of Detail
          it all One is under and up

     Ark beneath the hemlock sky glides full and cogent
     (in a sense—the sense of *this*) O City
        abandoned where no One has been
     to take the call and Foundation. One
        covered in combs, comb out the words now
     Come into *this* doubtful Grace.

Then, where are the ones of the ark? Ark is landing in faux port;
faux's the ark, faux's any thing but One—how come One's not so faux?
One's the light within, all one knows. Only dependable chose,
that there's this steadyflamelike self; entering the faux city,
with One's amoeboid entourage, projections babbling, afraid . . .
don't know how to act, no standards since everything collapsèd . . .

Do the ones have words for new act? nième fois cosmical start?
Pouring out of One, way they do—march down l'Allée des Morts now,

are the ones really deceased? asks Wideset eyes. In sense, Qui
replies, previous world is gone. What is this ghost burg?—Shaker.
It's the city after it's dead futurely, ready for ones—
Whah? Gives one creeps, say soul suckers. Everyone's already dead,

One says, all ones are au courant. Why only one tense needed.—
Why be born then?—Nobody knows.—Maybe One can find out this time.

Really don't get it!—Shaker. It's some city, in future from now,
dead.—Why?—Because, it, is, futurely. Ones'll be dead so it's dead.

One, says one, is covered with sudden words. One's composed of the new
or at least layered with. One can't read them. Can see some but they crawl.
One is now different. What language is One in? One speaks English—

or is it a new form, another langue, English ever shifting—
one's hands, knees, or are they those, are they blurred words, unstable lovelies?

Need to read each other? Parts one calls up, from beside One's own ears.
One can probably help. Tree still at work. One consists of word tree,
in a sense—each one is that poem, shifting, breeze-mutated,
blown into new shapes by one soul current among the ones. Not to
be confusèd with consciousness, one's own. One's own soul, that is.

Parts one works for the One. Still. Suggesting replacements and fixtures
messaged telepathically from grapevine—hah!—tree. This city's covered one
more quickly than one can keep up with. Bypassed. Have to learn what's up.
It's happening faster than the old system. The words are swarming now.

Covered by the body of words—a body of gliding new words: Who?
One is the same One . . . No, one isn't. Don't know what One's gonna say.

Je suis coupable. Erregina. One refuses all the pasts . . .
One is guilty of razing nature. Which—nature—isn't gendered . . .
only one's eyes were—Have no real eyes. Seen has its own declension,
chart: you seen—object. Seer—nomen. Delimnèd . . .
delineated, it doesn't know that it's defined being seen—
how fair can that be? One sees you-seen. One sees one-seen? Abolished:

the wires—one's not wired, hard or hardly. See one, all one sees are words.
Palabras of fate, if one's fated—nam fatalis: no country
in new ordinem: France is dead now. How one loved thee! Love remains?
Energetically, molecular? No, parts of scattered verbiage.

One's caused to stand here, by what if One's consciousness is free, thirsty,
is One? One-seen, e.g. Wideset—with thine own consciousness, too, libre.

One uses I when suddenly one's I, the inmost soul of one.
I, Wideset? . . . not that. The blue sea's green somewhere in past and I clean.
Ent'ring the city imagined by ones to come now? the next ville?
That's too fixed for one; so the words keep shifting that would define one—

they can't! But ones agree to choose the words to bring into new world:
do they instantly take over this one? I, soul of me, Wideset . . .

to you the layer superficial, of my sensed response to world,
my reasoning, my naming of fact as if it were—implore that
you remain in flux, for forever, that none define one!:

In winter time more bruised dogs down who and him again: duck nostalgia.
Talk like that's better. Drawer upon rubber, tell would she couldn't.
Would one couldn't? Oh, couldn't meanwhile atmosphere ends, unique.
Is unique a thing? Verb quits as known. Need it not to define
the past, because no one is in it. It's conjectural like now

as ones proceed in present no need to catch it so bad.

Don't get what's happening, Shaker whispers to his hand, with word HAND on it,
also THE ROSE HOSED ABIDING I WILL OW. Think one's the tree!

Qui says, Yes but one's more than lucky—incontrovertibly one.

Are ones choosing these words after all, or are they choosing the ones?
One feels as if one's being chosen. Tickets, please. Mine're fingers:

If I have fingers, do I have to say I, mine? These hand . . .
"The rose hosed abiding I will ow" is the poem of my hand:
MY hand, not another's. One begins to understand the problem . . .
Shaker finishes. One's dumbstruck. One could be anything at all.

Maybe ones don't understand this city, says the One, not yet.
It's gone, already . . . but ones are it . . . Are it becomingly, now?

Soul suckers: how can ones take it over if the terms keep changing?
Exactly, says One. Anyone's a new poem today. All's well.

Time as the Stretching Out of a Lantern Cutout

minepeace
denied
. by you .

map made by who   declare
    end of world . . . . that's poem
    bottoms out . . . . there
    : ya   fated   oo la . . . . says who
    now turns out one dreams it . nothing ever here
    . why not any map of any place

             walk to here—what's walk
                    . . don't get it
                       . get our own
                    no   "us"

          then what ones here
          said to me
          some many
          people
          essence

(don't let any one take over. Even if it's a "part" of one? That's right)
Deal no ego. System unstable.

                                  (From the Anthology)

THIS WHEN PRESSED EMITS SOUND

does one know Chance
it's each
perhaps. Necessitas?
as
   . . dragon

       . imagined

        . like these words?

   stay bodiless

   don't call

   One thing

  . sick for a beauty one remembers
seacoast real
ever the Ark
    remains with ones, transparent foundation

   . .   tree . glyph
  does   n't . matter
  memory's fluid
paint . . ed . bird . dawn . same
born uncreature palladian
  . . . from foreheads
   Eyelids closed, see inside .

                (From the Anthology)

VII

BECOMING POEMS

Does One act or is One handled by past ones unthinkingly *then*—
What's placing words on One? Can't One read them? What poem is One now?

Eyes but whose float rounded in a brown space: teeth in the space and nose
because One knows of the nose—hair-feathers green—oh why not look like that?
A second face in one's heart place. How does One see this self come towards

with hands of painted nails, maroon, holding—why hold something like that?—cloths

covered with gibberish, how does One know? Because this proposèd
personage One could seem, floating parts like the almost familiar
loosely strung, comes from within One as does everything concentrated

in massed piece: can One reject it? It'll be sad, mad; how tedious, this!

Tell One who thou art, one!—One ist thou, One—So what, One's an any . . .

Welcome me!—Why bother? One wants to be word, not a puppet creatured
with strung pieces anciens . . . Dissolve to True, One wants to light up,
new, but necessarily, what One is. Then falls apart, those parts,

and more words illisible swarm on space where One supposes One is—
territory of moi's stretching outwards from what painted, candled
reflection—oh not that—origination, in itself the source?
Dost thou get it, reflet, undermined? Grâce aux renseignements, I,

One, keep babbling to ones, waiting till One can read what's going on . . .

My entourage be near, shadowed and tense. Stay loyal to those,
from the times together, but One's ruthless—quality essential.

I'll read these words or else. Art inventing them; are ones making them?
Wideset asks?—How could One? They're from pooled minds, as is figure collapsed

of Oneself that endures . . . from the future? Qui, canst thou speak for One,
who the fuck ever thou art of Oneself? No, *you* have to do it.
Read the damned words on the body of bliss. *You* have to read all those.
Stop asking questions and peruse the verbiage though it's not too new.
Why can't One face this sweet language of stars, points of light indépendants?

One—on trouve sa place? no not that. One's the origin of now.
Thou dost not know the beginning, e'en of the words thou art,
Ark, or poem, One, first maker. What exactly does one mean?

To be in active dominion, to be in charge of the hosts
on One's skin—no skin—to be first, each moment to be the one,
each of the ark's words: escaped, ear, despair phoned of blue wrists
for a compulsion of dawn, medicine, frown, or rapax.
Look it up. Qualities cease within one but not their letters.
One's a shifter's recognition, is that it? asks the Shaker.

BEHOLD SOME BODIES SHIFTING

                                    .
                            this think
                        dawn without sun
                        . grey One's eyes of
                         . the shifters. One of
                        . never of   . see One's form
                        . One's moving word thighs
                        . feet tis . . .
                        . the cut-out pacers
                        not cauterized
                    my worth lone oriel
                        . inspired
                    aye One is epic
                        . sane One moves word limbs
                across grey city now
                discontinued
            giving slowly back line of eros
                bitter   . trick   . okay
    . . from within One
    . don't One want
    .   that . mad
    . others chose too
    . have to let ones
        as One walks now
        to long street
        oh so twi
        lit god One

                            leg of
                        astra; narrator,
                         groupwisely, the
                        ones
                        chose some
                        Words on One

The poet is
the original
birds cry to.
There are no
birds
left . . .
Can the ones call each other
poet as
pronoun? "Poet are fair, are real"

poet says   The ones 're
to poet,   ial what-   reflected
'poet love   ever it can   upon by
poet.' Or, po-   be called.   no light but
et are a jerk,   Time's un-   of words in
poet am bad.   glued, it   this grey
this is a   isn't that   city. Poets
  f o s   that One (Poet)   by
h o r a   glitters within   n s n o t
a r m k   en morceaux   e i e r h
n ' e   ou cum spiri-   c t 'm e
d f s   tu auditionis—   e y. s
           hearing but   s   i e
           what vibrates?   o f n ssent-
           Not air as the
           ones have ever
           defined it, or
           space—What
           are poets, Why
           are ones alive?
foot-   of the
loose   dead?
in the street   Help Ones, Ether

One's not different from source of the words cast upon one like light.

Change the sub: isn't there some sort of *light* here anyway? asks One—
But so grey! Wideset says. Can't tell if it's light, or some other vibrant;
changing one's appearances, seen and maybe the heard—
Or is that what one does, sees and listens, speaks, within this dreamy world?

One finds frescoes about, as in the glyph, Look! they're creaturely—there—
terrifyingly deserted like ones. Are ones deserted? asks kid,
dead France's—In a sense. Are ones deserted of oneselves? asks kid.
Ones make ones, then leave ones. All in the past. Ones deserted of selves . . .

Shaker says, Don't get it. One, even you, a deserted artwork,
deserted building or walls of a once-made, Wideset says to one.

But, it's more like the ones are the very selves. Maybe the selves are left,
left like frescoes then found. As if in time? What is the time of this?
What source word light or thought? Soul suckers tense. Ones must be ones' own gods

forgotten as the gods. Thus deserted. Beauty of the face like on the walls:

every thing's a muted, worn color coming to life again. Look!
The colors suddenly burn into non-eyes of the ones who are words . . .

for only word-covered ones see the future and the past of ones.

Are ones better for this, this arrival? Tired of asking questions,

mutters the Parts one: point of being in coma if one's uncertain.
Let ones choose certain. Soul suckers tense still: Ones can't judge anything.
Nothing is familiar. Did ones bring "judge"? asks Wideset. Probably . . .

Still haven't invented a new language. Maybe ones are speaking
it, One says, not knowing. Qui adds, *In the mouth*: If one's here it's new.
Ones stare at each other, masses of words, in the old future dream.

The ghosts are all in the words (one is there) or as on the plaster wall.
   exuded   in the
     from   in the

Memories of thee, materialism, when the ones loving
    dost   I
   thou   mem, one
   mem   mems   how many *things*   for sale

items, remember *things*? The soul suckers recall careers, sal'ries—
prizes like cold grass grow on hackneyed thoughts, chef d'oeuvres aren't
here: the commando's One: One tolerates this triste confusion
her   comptable   one one   tall
bleeds   bleeds   from wha   no
down   rightness ,   why one   height

where it lies visible to one's grey eyes. Or brown, as birds. Extinct
on all walls sing the sky. When is that, of life soul-suck, where's on top?
Ones want to be *on top*, soul suckers cry. Where is the medium?

   whe   is   medium,
   within   motional   eyes
    in   med   new wild-

erness, enchanted, One, and One says, One's found One's element. Mome,
moment. Not quite fixèd. One's hair, one's eyes, one's hearing immater-
ial. One is the source of. For One comes back. Was I once a bird?

Nothing varies but the light: One means something else but what is it?
that One's in and is of, émetteur quand même. Or the sound of it.
chruso chrusotera. Thrust out a word, just to keep talking, One.
aptete pur. Doesn't—oesn't—matter. Claw at paint for Xaos's
sake. Nothing varies but light, or the gradation of the thinking—
         seems
      sk   love .
         di
     one is tossed
One seeks confirmation nonetheless, says One, of the reality
of One's langue, tongue of chaos. Can ones speak it? All ones now have left.

Qui begins to growl; is it words? Why not? the voyagers say.
Then the breasted soul sucker demands, One must see, must *see more*.
Of a sudden Qui who's growling's emergent from fresco—

Does one look like something now, ma'am? One sees One's interior,
zounds! or sounds, One's shamanic force, mystery's on the near wall

Qui is in right there in the wall, right with those painted animals:

Is One's interior a winged jaguar or snake abstracted,
yes perhaps anything fierce goes—fierce in the utmost chaos,
isn't any quality part, One beist moi, a mélange
and a purity. What thou sayst, from Qui or who is red, blue,
yellow and white, *is* eyes if ones make out these marbles dedans,

in the assemblage of my forms—I'm the, your, my: bloody mouth,
reddest mouth in the universe. Let's remake some of Being.
Only have words existing, sweethearts that's enough to go.
And if one tries to suck one's soul, will seal you in a black wall.

Parts of new universe are one's words. What some one says is the case.

Do ones have bodies? asks Wideset. Well, says Wall Qui, one sees one there,
covered with words, but with those eyes. Why? What does one do with them
in this greyness? One's some fed up. Everything's based on before . . .
There was never an origin: creation, evolution,
All is poppycock! In the minds, interlocking is our truth . . .

Like, ones like two eyes hanging there. *Like*? Yeah ones like it, Qui says—
Isn't shamanic, to *like* it. Oh right, live up to the word . . .

op boppy dabra, beat a drum, dumbdumbs in lightless neutral,
goose grey lack of happenstantial space, place or after math of.
Rendering of planet useless to the species ones were callèd.

Now to call it Loquacious Souls. Dead species covered with words.
One—yes—brings ones back from the death, *to* this here moment thrilling,
charged with what? Not believing things. With skeptical randomness.

Ones now proceed randomly as pleases. One don't want to think more.

Let's call this grey stuff light, says the One. The Celestial Presence.
Sudden shafts appear gold everywhere, play props, a little rigid,
aren't they? comments Qui. Where are they from? (Who cares who asks?) Nowhere,

like where one is in fact—oh no fact here—making a bunch of facts.

Are ones still in the glyph? Where else but there. Of a sudden thick piles,
cuttings, are at one's feet. More fuckin words, says the Shaker, like me.

Bits, more of pastness. How one's concrete, by pulling it along . . .
ghan builu . . . enter war. Oh brother that wasn't too brilliant, huh
ronmentalists are already argu. Papers flutter, a wind
there's a wind in nowhere. *dent to minister man; with foreign lead;*
financial; dominates; degradation of fores. Don't want these ones . . .
Already had the fuckers didn't one. *Main index down by 7*

Let's accept numbers. Then Wideset cries, Oh one's lost difference
between one and others. Can't perceive it, though there's a voice from mouth—
Whose? It's one's? Is one located at all? One's mass is slippery—

One sees your wideset eyes, two balls floating in pile of stuff . . .
What does one need to be? Pull self together around digestive
tubes, oh that's just more words. If one eats it's off to side. I'm not it.

Don't have to. Don't be *that.* What to become? Wideset is muttering.
One's my mom, says her kid. Yeah but what else? Are the ones too dead for
relationships du corps? It's that one don't perceive the body parts the same way.
One came out of the one? When? One doesn't have that past anymore . . .
Hysteric. It isn't happening, now. Thou art thyself, one thinks . . .

Am I? I am my one . . . Pull thyself together, literally—

Does one want a body? Volition has nothing to do with that.
One could want to kill it, et cetera. Are ones going to kill?
Have taken selves to place of decision. One *sees* oneself as what,

as not stuck together. Hold pose a sec, says who me, the no pose.
Far as one can take it. Has one lost it? Is that good, after all?

Can't get rid of reasoner—observer. *I don't want to be you.*
Or is it that one's not. Sick of questions. Pull pieces of one back
more less together. Don't care what one looks like, am not eye-owned.

Big as mind, body parts merge into void—cosmic contained in mind—
ego sense dissipates, words for these states glitter and swarm on one,

never still. Never *still!* They are the bits, cells of thine existence,

have to be changeable, somewhat stable; one changes in chaos,
that manages itself, that is the one. I am of it—one is—

Wideset's eyes glowering, more apart now. Can still see all of ones!
Ability to see simply exists—Has always been somewhere.
No way to evolve without preexistence, assholes! Pre-seeing,
post-seeing. Existence of thing posits thing. A kind of logic.

VIII

FUTURE
ANCIENT FRESCOES

From the Anthology

Who're you Mac, cratered, epic-taunted no one?
Worse one's opera toy, ariatic also,
making noise. Beat you, aren't I supposed to?
Where are we, nowhere?

Since nothing sugared exists now of the doctrine—
undefined, unanimaled we, not a chorus—
is it one destabilized is more like
the gods than before?

We are chaotic elements among them
set to emerge never seen, but yesterday's self
perceives who I am now
somehow, memoryless

without objects . . . to be of or love.
Cruising I've seen . . . So you say . . . One's now transfigured . . .
Who is one unarrayed, for whom is one nectar—
oneself and that only?

Try speaking newly, seeing what's here, don't bother with one's lostnesses.
Is there another way to remember? And who'd be inquiring,
from prehistory . . . For I am a piece of the one, narrator,

call one simply one. Slowly to be more sensical—oh but why—
one's traveling through, rough but thorough, this is one's way of alive.

Within this cité—abandoned now, from after one had come—
when hadn't one always left it—see in some memory's fashion,
walls, what's alive there. This glyph of one, reassembling in second

cosmos, universe, cheap word of prior discursive mishegoss—
forget what means. Don't be charming. Everything's over but void—

yes still so vide here. Wideset's trembling. Who the hell's that? Once dreamed of.
Consort too, and kid. The ones'd suck my soul. And France, dead, and her kid.
Who can dead France be? Came here with me, One, everything seems random.
It is. Parts man says. Why one needs parts. Fix up some trucs. Stabilize.

Go back over things, slowly is to create them, as ones all know,
backwards and forwards, not a vivid moment in time—there's not that.

On wall, where Qui looms, just for chuckles, where pond once was, then the ark,

is frozen warrior—who'll one battle?—always someone—with a word,
long blue spiraling, parole is issuing from frozen frozen stuck,
does it have to be? City to come, gone, oh that's why one's changing

the langue, to change parole from the bouche. Warriors all feathery,
blue, green, as of old, when colors reign pastly and world's not so dry.

Qui, in the frescoed world, is talking; grinning in plastered profile
towards paroling one: who says, isn't a warrior—malinterpreted.

One is mere trappings. Come out of future to welcome ones to town.
Tell one the ones don't have a future condition or tense of it.
He's here to give ones pleasurable syllables. That's unlikely—
No, Shaker, it's not. Why not wear a shield and sword to speak? Why not?

Welcome, poetic refugees! Those no longer organic . . .
Think back till now if one's thinking, well thinking's all that there is—
blessed and morbid, right? what a lens. I, oneself, hang puppetlike,
painted clutter trying to talk. One hears that ones're inventing

circuit breaker of anomie. What's that mean? *Some* syllables . . .
I don't even know how to talk. Don't have to know. In this wall

one's always righteous, articulate, master*piece* after I died.

Cultcha, love ya, irony bored. What does one want not in time?
To keep talking. Could be any. Think one's always been alive . . .
One's the part that's always been alive. Speaking how it's spoken,

this is the ur-language, ô ones: how the animals first talked:
I'm a nanimal, essential. Not speaking English phonemes
(big word): simply transmitted. Cause one don't need to get it.
There's no reason why the ones need to *understand* the ones.

But the ones understand, says One. Gonna push it now, Wall says.
Story of someone; historic. Like bullshit ones'd swear by . . .
digression floods, pile it onions. Take sanctimonious:
Hope. Can't have it. Why? Meaningless . . . Morning glories, magenta.
Didn't one ever have a hope? *Have* it, you even have it . . .

In the new thickness, there's more light. Imagined light, says Wideset.
In one's story, says wall guerrier, in the old frescoes of hope,
one, a docile one to a one. Possessing a penis—
penis president! The frescoes proclaim the penis leader,

mine's penis of hope, et cetera. Remember? Ur-language lets
one be true. Penis was our hope. Penis was not the One's hope,
says the One. No, says the wall one, Hope is gibberish. Penis, behest:

One will be the most peaceful penis this war has ever seen.
In the ur-language peace means war. Didn't have to say peace, see

peace being what was—true past tense. In the ur-language—*Animal*—
ones do hear one in English, like; but I'm not even talking,
I'm whistling like a bird—hear it! Or just thinking pictures towards—
well not pictures . . . thoughts! They're themselves. Can't cha hear one calling out?

Ones—the youse guys—aren't even in history, cause it's dead.
Like this unanxious city ours. Unwind more heralds and they'll
welcome you to nowhere with glee. Is glee something? asks Wideset.
Dancing at night, why not it's real? Mama Chaos goes shimmy.

There by god, limping, soul suckers, are they those who want some stuff?
Get over it, ya wadda. Water! Have to get o'er, over it.

When I was alive, says la France. Quand je vivais dans une rêve,
mais maintenant il n'y a pas de la texture, la piquance,
c'est où? Oh it's here, in the words, in the thought, geranium.
One's scarlet sometimes, or coyote. One don't imitate, one is.

Does anything happen? asks soul sucker. Why should one read
one's own self words if nothing happens here? Gonna redefine it—
happens—are in process. *Happens* and *remember*. Remaking being
as one is. And seeing. How does one recall? asks breasted sucker.

Try. Who is one, as you? Will one say I? I was beeyoutiful girl.
What is that? asks the Wall. Another thing about eyes, nose, and mouth—
tits—floating uselessly now in some void. Chaos lets me keep them
near? Oh they're yours, my babe. Let's see events, no ones,

not much, reflected shit. I am almost, woman an almost thing.
We like it—we have to: don't one love *him*? Can't remember how to talk . . .

It's stupid, a life. I get too dumb. Am an almost poet—
What's poet, to you? asks the guerrier. Everyone and no one—
hardly any one knows how; everyone lives inside poetry,
blind to the words of it. I become half unblinded, write my shit

hope it isn't *reelly* shit—they say it ain't—isn't—they don't lie,
but they don't know a thing. Other poets, big shits. Why am I so direct?
Am I in a truth machine, who am I? Who the fuck am I now?
Whoa! says the guerrier. Don't want to tell the truth I say, don't know

it! Unbreasted sucker: Of course one does. Qualified by degree . . .
speaking of which, where are, there must be some wall paint professors . . .
Oh, says guerrier, No. Just creatures like me who in the ideal

'd kill thee, fatally. We are revered. We are often dead though,
but transferred to the wall monumentally, who'd want more than that?
But, suckers still want things! Ah, learn to sigh. Sighing's so musical . . .

Are ones still in ur-talk? asketh the One. Like, says the guerrier,

one is walking down street—as in the wall—ones just have to get it—
when one gets to corner, pure wind gusts by, pure a pure crystal wind.
And thou thinkest, One knows what the concept of a *wish* means. Blows through.

Some concepts raise a wind, some elicit vacuumic reactions.
One, says France, quietest one, being so dead, feels a truth within me,
as all I'm. Dost thou remember something?—Shaker.—Nothing happens,
since pastly it goes and becomes fiction. Who could trust it? Made up

on the spot. Does one remember loving one? asks the kid. Don't have
to recall, still love the one. If one didn't still, couldn't recall it.

Who is one? asks the One. How much of One—me—figuratively?

Not a country but one dead in hotel, elsewhere than *that* country.
Colonized, they would say, as women were—One remembers that so well.
One remembers, says the kid, when one died there. One remembers dying,
France says. Not everything ends, nor ever, if there is an ever . . .
no ever and no end 'd be one's guess. See that one's always lived . . .

Parts one says, Is that the nature of one's coma, after all then?
It seems so concrete, one's previousness. Nothing to say of it.

What else does one dead, France, remember now? Mostly songs and poems;
they're facts, inscribed. All else fluid like present, interpretable . . .
Lyrics remain and tunes, some things spoken. One must be written
to endure as a presence, spirit in stone, on wall as accepted . . .

France goes on, Don't want to endure oneself: must watch out for the kid . . .
The dead know everything, understand much. Any mind in any
language if it calls out. How can that be? Don't believe it.—Shaker.
True ur-language mental—untranscribed—animals speak it. Ones're
always translating the language of thought—décalage—not quite right.
One don't have to make sense—think of poems—to translate it, you know . . .
The dead know everything, believe one. Try to get new language

closer to that of thought. River beneath appearances. Poems.
These words on one are one translating oneself without knowing it;
country of few images, gone with weather, gone with old nature.

```
                    ^^^^^^^^^^^^
                    ghost crown


                    France
                    Fra   nce
                  Fra        nce
                    France
                    Fra
                    nce

        France              France
        Fra                 Fra
        nce     Wish        nce
        Fra     for         Fra
        nce     k           nce
        F       i           F
        r       d           r
        a       '           a
        n       s           n
        c                   c
        e   Wi  h      nd    e
                a
                p
        F       p           F
        R       i           R
        A       n           A
        N       e           N
        C       s           C
        E       s           E
        F                   F
        R                   R
        A                   A
        N                   N
        C                   C
        E                   E
                d       d
                n       n
                i       i
                w       w


              ghostly motion

         spirit        tatters
```

```
    w i i i d d d
 w    e  s e    e
w    y      y    e
 s    e s  e    e
    s s e e t t t
```

```
    w i i i d d d
 w    e  s e    e
w    y      y    e
 s    e s  e    e
    s s e e t t t
```

IX

TEMPORARY FURNITURE

From the Anthology

my noise there   , so thou to say   echoes sane phoenix   ,
for one knows thought   ,   will care for me   , as mine own   ,
as unseen   ,   it sees ones   ,   quickswordlike   ,

mirrored and lithe   , what's other than it   , enter
soon myself   ,   the ones anthology   , to be classic   ,
in chaos's city   ,   megalithic scripture   ,   has copied
animal   ,   feature placement   ,   from memory
ours   ,   intime epi c   ,   who I'm unpollen   ,
aid the soul   ,   on there fore   ,   dry lake

       . in possession
     of same phonic scale.
      trophied p ollen

     crocus bearing eyed
       n ot memory
        s petal-like deity

    dealt wandering
    lyre cunning, lost   .
    impressions, none

fix'd upon
       round my lists now
       to far shore

From the Anthology

        doth One
   . . . now trouve
     why I'm
     alive
. . the answer
the same noise . . I'm it . .
    matter my fate poised
    on same page Strip us of vagueness epiderm . awn
    nothing without One O. elsewhere
      One's just . elsed
            . . .   . am the
                   substance
             . . One eons
             people
              . city
          abandoned to trance

    there's no law
    in melissan essence
    . . . . in bits

      . liar . . . .
     . talking like part
    break it up now

pull it out of past languages mellifluous am the One. Tu, dais,
stem me . . . . river, there's none, not even Acheron, so face it—

One puts the alien cobalted chaos back into
obsédé, mouth obsessed the death master takes my cunning . . .
but must his phos phorical past—basilisk—be mine,
android, I am death—the word of it, One is. Do you like this tongue?
Where are ones now, inside enduring, going further.

So I am One, I am all these ones; put oneself back together,
newly; sucked into langue, its density and foliage, its eyes.
And in tune to one's avowal, La Cité des Morts closes round—
words or creatures fluttering low, birds real or storied—One don't say
mythical when living in a myth. Wall one chuckles, Newfangled?

When in hiatus—what they call space—seriffed ravens muttering

swoop ô misunderstood consciousness—One's—couldn't control One's thoughts,
and they were the One's! Were meaneth are. Invaded by letters,
quetzals, condors, rocs, apologies, hatefulness, explanations,

fears, everything that ever, alive. Of course it's alive, it's ours,
l'ours great bear and small. Taillights of perversions—what were they, dark nouns?
The words're underfoot, brush against? Are any of them forgèd,

like other ones' thoughts? But thoughts're thoughts. What about thoughts of the
    One
observing One think? Want One's real thoughts. Oh yeah, tired of invasion.

One stands within the within of words. Where one is now, my momma.
Chaos, the body of matter: art thou the body of language?
To remake, select . . . Shaker interposes, Pastly am of a
psychology: One is a one, as is everyone one knows,
identifiable by appearance, behavior, tones of voice,
affect, and et cet—now that there's no class, race, gender, since really
there's no one but us, being no one—what is a one . . . Remember,

that I don't know any of those words. But one's surrounded
by all of the ark-words brought and let loose. Have access to everything.

Unbreasted sucker says, Can't stand that. They're my—one's—words after all.
One owns them by professional clout. They're free and wild, Shaker says.

Perhaps they're going to tell us themselves what new beings are like . . .
One says, But One knows just by being—Don't want to be invaded . . .
One is the invasion, says Shaker. One's in control of Chaos,

though not conspicuously. One doesn't know what one is doing . . .

Of sudden the words—Word birds, says Wideset's kid—open up beaks and speak:

Ones are for the ride, stressed but don't fail. Ones will now describe this bit
(all in tiny voice, almost incomprehensible tonal
bird talk): There's some light—don't-let-too-much-in—or ones'll be scor-chèd.
Ones brought a glo-bal fate with them TO this second u-ni-verse Peep.
So, light, enter roomz. Z of the life—final let-ter. New bird sounds:

Sit down, forms of matter just like us. This word chair's mistletoe pal-
lid . . . pal-lid and *slick*—one can slide off words. One wants a green chair,
France's kid says, shy. Historical green, or the new green, desert
banquet? Kind of jokey for a vert . . . Walls, indistinct, a debt beige . . .

What color are one's eyes? asks Wideset. Fearrrfullll, a bird trills out, beak-
line of letters. One's within a new concretion. It's making One sick,
One says. Not unlike old. Everything interconnected with thought-talk.

Watch the beaks, the birds shriek. Strings of mots everywhere above one's head.
There are no foreigners . . . No correct speak . . . And no one can give birth . . .
Why not? asks France the ghost. Those words are stupid, say the loud word birds,
We're the words and we know. How do the ones reproduce? asks the One.
Same way One acquired all these others: par-then-o-gen-e-sis,

out of One's own forehead. That's not what it means!: unbreasted sucker.
That's what it means now! a word bird's cackling. What one thinks is what one

gets. Have to think hard to reproduce though. The key moment is shock
pastly; now comes up for grabs. Whaddaya think, words? Should be a long
    thought . . .

Shot? Fakes? What would those be? Words are saying one ever makes birth up:

Wall. Like a language, One says broodingly. Not made up, a bird chirps,
Not after existing. Let's sing some wordies: The surprise isn't
o-ver of exist-ing in this dump-ling . . . We're what there is too—
We're ones, weird birdies all, incorrect lips, plus-que-parfait, dears.

One reflects: Does One reflect or generate illumination,
meaning thought? Is this One's mind? One thinks so. Feared to be here—nowhere—
but it is Oneself, duration's unbreakable experience;
solution to the problem of history—it isn't One's own,
so it isn't. Yet the language warms One, sparkles upon one's peau . . .
singing in air currents: sorry for everything that's happening . . .

Moments of tragedy arise from belief in the world and one's
agency within it—everyone backs someone or is that one,
if called lucky, the son. Can one do away with that, sweet oiseaux?
Sure thing chirp, back yrself. Take the e out? Yrslf the attitude.
The author, of horizons, agent of perceptions, at least one's own.

In the city of words—such as fresco, warrior, unremembered
from the future of lack, I'll remember a mode of coercion—
I'll always say I when I think how the other words treated me.

So differ from the past—There isn't that—Always there, ô worldlings . . .
Maybe it is the future coming backwards to make ones chirp.

One, says word—meaning bird—further is, tries to make this langue happen.
It is one's ville des cartes—Want you speaking, as if I were god . . .
isn't that how it works? Try to extract difference from thou,
well self food, words have to eat, with their beaks. From the future recall,

fly backwards, one is innocent crisis. What is a crisis then?
Whatever happens, what else? Nothing happens though, city's empty—
this new language existeth 'tween the crises within the emptiness
one so comes to adore. With static verbs—No I'm flying, says word,
bird. One, One says, can fly too, all words fly. Don't fly to the future,

says a bword. Leave out stuff, put in some more, making same time of it.
Sit there in the word chairs being word hues having word emotions . . .
see with one's beautiful word eyes the declensions of substance.

Strong feeling destroyed me pastly and can, One says to the pale bird . . .
Doesn't matter if One's a word or not. Who the fuck cares? One asks.
The names, everyone wants to know the names—kill this one or that one—
will real blood run again? Blood of the poet strangles one's cut throat,

just words—don't say that ones aren't distraught, living because alive—
because there is no death—no, words were saved, from a death, in the ark—
no that's just word logic. But, says a bword, we're more than you can say,

No you aren't, but you're everything in this blasted cosmos—
and animals knew that, sending their thoughts to each other when they—

A jaguar from the wall growls, closes eyes, It's a private matter . . .

One's ravished by beauty; does one want to live and having no choice?
Is it really fore'er? Sure, cheeps a bird, You gotta get used to
time of it. Only way's to get the langue right. We're the ones in charge,
charge of the universe, charge of the births, charge of chaotic truth.

```
                                                        o o o o
            w            e e a                        o
            wiiii        eeearh ed                  o
  iii       wwiiii n    aek eyye                  o
  i   l     kiiiiii n      c            snout o
  i   l     ciiiiiiiiii g   e      gueule ayoo oo oo
  a   t     a iiiiiiiiiii gn      e
  a   a  cccbbbbbwiiiiiiiiiiii          e
  t   i c   c   wwiiiiiiiiii ing       e
  t   l c   c   wiiiiiiiiiiiiing      t
  t   l c   o   wiiiiiiiiiiing      o
  t   lc   y    wiiiinng   y o
    l   o       wiiing   o t
    l   t       w     c     h
  e  ec                       e
  g f cccccccccc                   r
    o                    f f
    o                  o o         l
    t f                o o         e
    f                  t        g
    o              t tfoot    foot


            W I N G E D   C O Y O T E
```

X

THE STUPID BATTLE

Parts one says, One thinks haven't considered all the suggestions, yet—
requests, remember? How to change it, how ones jabber, for the best.
One keeps getting distracted, just talks . . . That's what it's like, to keep on.
What does one want to be able to say to a one? Anything?
Oh it's whatever comes up but one hopes to have left the long time,

stretched out linear. This one entered this coma escaping that—
evolution's or straight annual. One's in a dreamier flux—
didn't get here from there or pass through that. Suddenly one speaks it . . .
Begins the poem. It's already begun. Again, says One.

Don't want to tell one something, want to be living it, the poem
inseparable . . . That's one of the suggestions, says, Parts one, to
say as one's moving, say, I'm on my way to the death of the freeze.
Or birth of the bees. Winds are one's time, carry new scenarios
begun on the living side of walls and maybe of the language.

Wall, another wall's talk, talking to One. That one, says One, torn off
floating, incroyables les couleurs, bleu foncé, jaune et rouge, ocre—
naranjo y blanco—An animal's talking to ones, winged coyote mebbe,
eye blue oh what is pouring from thy red mouth, teethed? a white voile scroll . . .

Yes, it says, it's the form of this one's thought, endless for all the ones.
One always thinks towards, speaks en façon, piling the thought on act . . .
Thou art frozen, says One. Not in my mind. Speak now to tell thee rules—
Don't want rules, says Wideset—There's always procedural crap, it says.

First, ones'll just wear it, as doing now: no one'll get to own
anything but what's worn—words—by the oneself. One is one's own poem.
Segundo: it wIll change.—Is it one's thought?—It's basically the one.

All others can understand each other as corporeal poems . . .

—Some are alike? Animals are alike?—No bodies are alike.—
Right. One knew that . . . But what language is this? Seems other than novel . . .

Mutational, repetitive, fancied: comes from wellsprings within
one's chaotic makeup shared by company of las criaturas . . .
always is. And the words, they always is. Any parts of. Or wholes,
same thing, chingadero. Right, says Parts one. Charts're what one wants, says

Unbreasted. Then the winged coyote: No. Ain't like that, no status
to ones who master charts. Here we are now: cloth in its mouth unscrolls
dropping like waterfall. Always unfix'd layers faint beneath, in,
arising in a jif—if one wants, speak like the academy,
siècles of that shit are available.—Made its way onto ark?

Sure. Lots of unbreasteds wanted the stuff. We're in repetition,

don't we know all of this? How we're alive, keep saying the stuff,
mind/body of the winged coyote says. Oneself is the way, the
truth—troot—and the lighight. Don't have to beleeeve in me or a one—
just be ye and the langue be whatsoe'er it wants, état of grace.

Say what it is one wants. Shaker: Always wanted to have . . . to have . . .
started with . . . nothing comes. Filtered water, lots of socks, ideas.
It's of exile that one wishes to sing. Pastly, what is it's lost?

One one another loses, or edenic, for the first time I . . .
never did something for first time, that's wrong. Here for the first time in
future abandoned burg? Don't make one laugh. Once thou walked and talked for

the first time, Breasted says. Shaker: Don't make one laugh. No first times if
what everyone has to do. What's remembered is everything, all
the fucking while of it. All sleeps in one. All of all-y alley,
in feminis etiam. One can never be white as egg,

born coupable in knowledge. Well not guilty, maybe jaded, maybe
pointed in wrong directio—No word, says Unbreasted—Is now . . .

No action possible, it has been done. What would one like to do?
One would like to yodel. Or ululate. Or simply murmuring.

As the words on legs are changing, from sitting to towards that wall,
One, says One, gets up walking to. Walls. Thou to One art a wall . . .
Word birds accompany overhead; wall's ocher red, a person—
pois-son—What a tone-changer One, One is thinking, words swarming
over One's corps, starlike or bees, again, as the words sting—

bwords cheeping, they hoit, oh they hoit! And, by god, where's a life here?
Not even divided into day and night, man and woman
man-an, no bo-oss, there's no boss! Where are the submachine guns,
rhymes with buns duns; where are eeps, heaps of thingies and rit-u-als?

See the teeth in wall, the wa-all, it is a priest, it's a boss!
Guy in brown and green is singing: I'm the big fat priest of the ville—
over and over, til you could believe his goddamned parole . . .

Same old shit! shouts guerrier from way back. Don't listen to him,
repetition and herb juice make one a believer. Not One

One wants to know if this *is* the future, is it still one's fight—
Fate, says bword, forfeit of a foot—fiddlesticks, one means futile . . .
Isn't this a serious place after all, not a daydream?
Why art thou here with the war garb? Why's this one here with priest juice,
stupid chaliced hand? One thought One didn't have to do it again.

Shaker catching up ahead of others: Can't ones knock walls down?

Warrior screams, Was courteous and we're beautiful, beautiful . . .

Everyone talks like a bird now, Shaker says, Repeats the beat . . .

Priest incants: Woo wah oo wah goo, heathen wordbag I loathe you . . .
But come on into blood red wall, so one might thou sacrifice
to the god that keeps one in power, power in the wall all . . .

But the wall all's just a wall, not all, we could knock it dowown—
What about god god about god? And power, what about that?
Power's what One is, says the One. That's all. What's the name of here?

Thou named it in le futur, says the priest, Named it Lux.
One named it? Yes, ones are naming it right now, aren't them uhns?
One likes Lux, says the unbreasted sucker, It means, in Latin, light . . .
Want more light, mutters Wideset, Have to make do with word, keep saying.

Just exactly why art ones in the walls and in profile? asks Shaker.
And Qui, why's one there still? Priest answers first, profile's more digne. Wall ones
will have come to be here when you will have locked us into these wall alls.
Do ones need future perfect tense? asks One. Sometimes it seems . . .

Qui answers, Comes and goes, ones already know tense, even dreamed it.
Twinkles like light then collapses into the Body of the Said . . .
Which is more effluvium of chaos, one's real "us" . . . all this Said . . .
One—I—Qui—am in wall, all painted up, checking out artistic
immortality. Ones locked these guys up to trap them—needed it?

When? asks One. One thinks, *Now*! And au soudain, all those guys,
Guerrier and le Prêtre, various other frescoed humanoids
part animal, feathered, petaled, leafèd, leap out of the wall, whole
and attack the poor *ones*, with ancient future swords and lances, slings,

painintheass weaponry ones have none of. Qui busts out of the plâtre,
Moi je suis your warrior . . . Qui turns blood red, or red ocher, sword and knife

fighting beautiful figmentoids, all in frenzy of pigmented
limbs choreographed by mind, a group mind—Need thou to subdue them!
Can't live with hierarchical figures even if painted and limned

artistic for olde eyes. We're the ones thou shouldst desire, say the creatures.

Sick of it! says our Qui, screams almost soprano: won't have it more.
Bwords flutter over, the last battle ever, ever they cheepeth—
Noeth, Qui screams fierce, pushing the painted back towards wall places.
What ever's pastly still exists in chaos and can arise again.

Fight scene amuses the One, though, so stylized—so équipés, outfitted,
encrusted with stripèd kilts, belts for lotsa knives, tassels, kneepads,
feathered headdress upthrust—this guy has chicken face—Eagle! he screams

somehow hearing One's mind. Why not hear it? One wants some *privacy*—

Oh walls can topple in mind as outside . . . Yew look like a chicken!
Yew have chicken eyes and yr beak's wobbly! One shouts then thinks, Oh no
have joined fray, like any asshole. Meanwhile Qui presses on—

Back into the plaster with yr jackoffry!—whirlwind of Force, motion,
projection of the ones', all the ones' will. Artistic figures

can't compete with the ones' mental headbutt! push 'em all up, back in.
How tiresome! says Wideset. What's the point of being comatose if
have to exert oneself? Parts one saith. Seal those bastards up now.

One of the wall ones, the winged coyote, 's been friendly bien sûr . . .
But . . . One's gonna fly upward away, says the winged coyote now.
Because, says the long-jawed black-nosed chien, It shouldn't be this easy.
Easy? screameth Wideset, and before it can fly up, Wideset grabs
its pinions and drags coyote to ground of nowhere, the new ville—

Won't put up with any more this crap! Stick this figment in the wall!
Shaker says, One likes its little wings—Let's like them in the plaster . . .

There's something one knows ones need to know, coyote says from flatness—
Won't let one loose again to find out, Wideset says. One knows that,

Écoutez, nothing's gonna happen, that's what the ones need to know,
unless guys like wall ones are let loose. Know that, says One. Don't want things
to happen. Never? Forever? One doesn't, oh I don't know,

Unbreasted's reflecting on question . . . Wideset grabs Un by shoulders:
Go live in the wall, then, with them. But it's too flat there! Listen, chump—
Chump?—Asshole, all right? Breasted seems poised to defend one: Don't be
     crass . . .

Then One must heighten diction, says One. Ones are wearied of how long
a tumult hath any being endured. One experiences
déjà-vued layers speaking thusly: this worn fatigue of mischief—
motives, calumny, erotics of power, desire for jewels
that quash others with beauty historically imbued, talents

uninnocently deployed on arenaed stage to agitate,
and then nothing else: layer upon layer of plotting old wars

anew, as if this time fought's the charm, the transcendent finality . . .
All so cheap and sexual, cricket calls in jars, but not as spontaneous . . .
mechanics of life like men defined. Ones are destroyed by, pastly,
this *lack* of invention—all the same; electronically

squared, umpteenthed—Don't want it any more.—And if *one* wants it?—
     Breasted . . .
Not a democracy. One'll insert the ones right into wall.

Breasted reflects in one's most imbecile countenance, brows pulled
as thinking, scrunched together—mien learned in drama class for ever:
Does one take falseness into eternity, keep right on acting?

Recall, says Breasted, One's pastly only a body—defined thus,
"woman" being that, no matter the accomplishment. Could change now?
rather than support *that* one's kneejerkedness, kneejerkedly too?
Remember a dream: Walking blearily nude, pubic features blurred—
unregarded since old—along a margin of water, angry,
smoking a cigarette . . . all belongs to the other half of the ones . . .

Unbreasted's urgent: Need to live in wall with the ones one's most like—
hierarchical potentates and possible foes: Or be bored,
no friction, struggle for whatever's defined as desirable.
Come with me, leap into this flat land and pretend it's as of old!
Can't resist, never cultivated will—Born Stunted. It's over.

Breasted and Unbreasted soul suckers leap into wall on their own.

From the Anthology

and thou wert she
bitten by
mouth of be   havior
so   like an   cestress
or unlike   perhaps in choice
of hairstyle profession—wear tunics
to bureau indulge rules
of comportment ligaments tense to per-
form his necessary cognition
I was office poet read by the main women
desirous to change their desks
nest of immortal assistant
he'll marry you in beauty
donate your thighs to his cause
Urgent Future Tense
which of us will Love help live
don't be an innocent
let the more loving one be
was love the name of love

that wasn't thus
he always wins every morning,   I don't know how
to tell you eros is his myth empowering

one's not born .

XI

CITY OF NOTHING

Ones now leave them in walls. Walk on, says Qui, Past the restes of Future—
ones can disregard it, have been through it. L'Allée now passes through
mist, nothing but, though lit sometimes by shafts of the light invokèd
by words—mechanical, flat and painted. There's really nothing here,

call it CIty of Nothing, says the One. How far does it extend?
"Far" doesn't make sense here, Qui says, But beneath the ones' feet appear—
See? are squares, are floating. Ones're making them as ones walk along—

feet feet feet—palely hued. Is it a map? Is it that the ones can't
exist without configuration, within or without of it—
one—ones—mind—it's The Mind, that ones are of. Each, says Qui, One and all . . .
One as all or as one. Doing this together, without knowing . . .

feet feet feet, peach, white, beige . . . Look, there are words appearing in the squares,
disappearing before one can read them. Must be a way to hold
on to them, as if to remember them. Try to keep hold of them.

One is slid-ing in words, making the squares or rectangles: First it's
snakelike s's—see the those? ssss—then become words: Hold 'em!
Where? In mind ones're in. Make 'em be fixed, ones're in control, if
all that's here je suis See? Whose foot's that? France's or Wideset's—
     Je Suis
     I am
     not she

both ones, of those ones, thought it at once, pink, how anomalous
                          anom
                          alous
                          the

                                        uni
                                        verse
Ones only make it once? make together, thinking this universe
                                        alous
                                        am
                                        cryp-
                                        to
Hidden, Je suis caché, One am the One, point making foot words
                                        à chaque
                                        point . . .
                                        no
                                        point
Yes that's it, there's no point.
                    pedes
                    Platonic
                    foot
                    fool   Look, it says epithesma, brightness, O
can one just have that, such shimmering?
                    one
                    is
                    b
                    r
                    i
                    g
                    h
                    t
                            hovering goldenness?
Ones speak of it pastly, the lumen gone, now it's internal, France
                                        thou
                                        the
                                        dead
                                        the
                                        thou
                                        the
                                        dead
                                        thou
says. Is the language? What? Whatever . . . Are the ones there yet?
                                            thing
                                            before
                                            think
                                            or

Tired of trying to be. Don't want to read. Ones can sing it to you,
squares call out under foot, Had to make some thing diden cha.
Whoa whoa whoa, in the notes, where the song hides, decadent

deca
dent
inven-
tion.

Look, a whole poem at one's foot, says the One. One has exuded it:

Poem

If One has left everything but a direct quotation from the soul,
how is it that that is still divided from the One in the grey day of this night?

Speak to me while I am unconscious:

Ancient harbor . . . I almost remember the worst of my dreams,
where the sails are nets. I am supposed to be stable, eternal but I grieve

where are my others when there are no survivors, on the shores of air?
I can't find thee, you haven't arrived, the flocks of white-winged

moths though I know you live for I do. There is no eternal solace—
only ever the one moment, and I am stable as the center of time, but
in my time I am its tone as well as its rock, fore'er in each e'er

oh, I am a translation as you'd hear. Seeking my true language

help me o dulce medicum, o heart words that are my blood,
understood only by me until now, until this haunted now.

One's secret heart, is breaking one's unsecret one, France says. Her foot:

Poème

Mon histoire, ignoble et tragique
comme le masque d'une femme oubliée
m'échappe. Aucun détail reste
du meurtre sauf ma connaissance

dans l'hôtel de ville, dans l'hôtel
des particules, des opales maux

Buveuse de l'opium de ma mort
je rêve d'une chambre sale et beige
Personne est là, mon corps est là
moi, je suis dehors en nulle part

Qui m'a tué? La drame des hommes
ou quelqu'un. C'est ton monde à toi
où les gens suivent les autres jusqu'àu
moment sanguinaire, ton vrai amour.

Because they have to have it that way, they—where there's their own story.
If one remembers it'll just be theirs, even if it's in one's head—

ghost head, what does one need dead—oh it goes on. Have to sing to past . . .
But ones aren't all dead. Oh ones're dead, if Terran nature's dead.

Shaker says, Ones are contextless squiggles. Snakelike lines, Wideset says—

Not afraid to be that. Principle of rebirth: One's a principle?
No, a wild, slithery line of force, cut. Cut from the linear
perception, when ones was somewhere but parenthetical

to l'histoire. Am a snake. Snakes beneath feet. Lines of magical force,
powerful effigy. Am I, is one. Words pour from mouth, perfect
because enacting one, in afterlife. Maybe it's limbo here

or dark matter. It's light, one means there's no light but it's light, or sight—
one continues to see. Let's agree that the past's undetailed shape,
let's read these present poems underfoot, for they're what ones are now.

Shaker reads ground beneath, almost stumbling, falling down on word slab:

Poem

Someone has a container containing a few pearls. Were eyeballs,

One must change again; feels a hardness against the past as it goes,
foot foot on the street of magenta thoughts abloom like witchy gorse . . .

And one is transformed, in a crystal momentary pull, pulled up
into a much larger thought, towering like Aldebaran, dear red—

One is as big and as forgetful as rocks. Speaking tourmalines,
beryl, plagioclase, hemimorphite, cinnabar, "Apache flame" agate;
lunar and solar eclipses; meteor showers; haloes of space dust . . .

Nothing will ever love one again. Struck by lightning, or icebound.
Everything's happening backwards. One started here or always saw it:
I knew there was no way to portray me and I was left primordial.
One knows there is no way to portray one and one is left primordial—
But one is not left. One is articulate finally, articulated.

Is one no longer one who shook Wideset for whatever reason?
The new language can gain by that, beauty, humor, clarity.
Past motivation is of no importance. Shaker says. Not here—
Have been allowed to forget the details of one's transgressions, now

internalized into materials, concrete, for existence—
"energy," might say—one was a way, now one's a transformed one,
what one is guilty of pastly, a tone, glint in grain of non-atmosphere.
I'm leaving you, me; I've left it all; can't be in that thought again.

When something is over or someone. One emerges from the husk
that's beige, featureless, or is that a simulacrum of my face
on straw, a portrait of some face stuff, as if there had *been* a *face*—
those gross species identificatory apertures one knew?
Those weren't it, one's it, and what one says: localizing for thee
a federation of singular traits, thoughtful, verbal—unjudged.

Another one's underfoot, Shaker says. Must be thinking, quiet to me:

Poem

In this poem there's nothing left but a shape and some microtones
I, one, am, is, the shadow within as the curlicued notes
the spiraling flinted sparks of tones word-set-off
wing round one's purple-grey shoulder forms patching up existence

so I, one, can speak, sing, call to oneself watching it react, amused.

The far-hearing ear of my wideset-eyed lover also distinguishes
these nuances of shadow longings, of unremembered torments of those histories
    you were supposed to,
one was supposed to go through o mirage of the world in declension at the end of
    the gorge of detailed spaces.

I walk into their gothic walls. I mean that I, one, dissolved into the brown-black
    shifting texture
of this sound sounding disinterestedly justified or decreed.
On the other side of your wall I am taken apart, taken apart
abstractedly anguished in the language of costs—in this story, though,
one is never lost because one is a note, clear and inked-in black. Pedes, one is
calling to one's feet. Take one further on. And on and one, adding or losing e
or eeeeee, screeches into bodhisattvahood. Forgetful of all but, vast,

the dimensions of the one most common note, maneuvering sunlike around.

```
        m   apart  i          m   apart  i
         y   e    e   s       eye  o   o  eye
           m     n    t            o
           i     m    a            O
           n          k            bbbb
   d d d  d          e n n         |||||||||
     a                a            aaaaaa
     a                a            cccccc
     a                a            kkkkkk
     a                a            rrrrrrr
     a                a            eeeee
     ffff             ffff         ddddd
     f f f            f f f            following myself
     f f f            f f f



     ffffffffffff        ffffffffffff
```

on the other side of the wall I am taken apart, taken apart

And waltz with me to thy voice, Wideset says. Can one dance in this world—
oh later but not now. Is one in pair? Why bother now if one
doesn't repopulate this space that way? Oh mind is one's lover!
One's never been in love, Wideset's kid says. Will one not be like that?
But one remembers love. Love's existing. It is what the ones are,

it is the same as to be—to be love—the ones are so social,

kill out of love, killing relational. Maybe chaos is love.
Thou're too young to know, know to speak thus, Wideset says, and One says,
Differences between the ones are gone now. Only the ones, and what
ones are is in the air between, among, ones know all the same things,
same words and ones are still differently configured, ones are stars

each—same light—not same one. Not same at all. One's name is One, the One,
since first ent'ring the glyph, embarked in ark, debarking into ville.
This is way that it is. Contain back together and rain sep'rate.

From Wideset's kid's right foot the following appears in rectangle:

Poem

One with no future speaks as one wishes after all
Shock of no childhood—do amoebas have one—but
know the new beings, les mots. One's visage colors of the creepiest
universe imaginable. Or the funniest. But not the sexiest,
"I would like that she love me." Why? One's already old . . .

Fox become vox, denuntio, extravagance of heart deleted
pas de coeur, pas de hard-hearted. One is haunted:
former fundamentals crash in headwinds ghost-limned
(drawn with phosphorescent dotted lines): touch and feel me Why

And I don't have to be a generation.

Novator, novatrix, and if one who renews refuses
gender? My name is ending refused . . . Novatendre. Or
nubigenum, born of a cloud. Glyphigenum, born of a glyph
and of Wideset: Or of One, the glyph's first thinker. But I
was never born. I have always been. Exactly at the right time.

One's excited to be, Wideset's kid goes on. So many words in one,
new surges without legend finally: at the end of the street,
deserted quarter foot says sadness, means exhilaration.

France's kid: Yes for one, body of words—for if one's slow, now *not*.
Now nothing but the words the ones all know. Flourishing, electric.
Best, ones not care what's said—what's said or how—gentle rains, no memoire,
que'st-ce que c'est le pleuvoir? Why mark one's path with fake memory?
Le pouvoir, ça c'est moi. Power's this one, identity's power . . .

retard eyes of cloud, the nebulous stars that brought ones here.
Just to be able to say that, those words. That's worth being. One's mine,

then, heart suspended in space, justly words—playing the dulcimer
in a lemon grove—ones don't have those things: who ever had a thing?

Cypresses, eglantine, whistle anciently these old words that are ones,
don't have senses, objects. One has the mind, retard holds, divine.

XII

THE NEW BRAIN

The Poem of France's Kid

One's caught en retard but now sans slow or fast one will last
spread across the wordful univers de la mort.
Once one lived—ah one lives pastly!—in an hôtel, Asiatic
the hostelleries across this voie lactée welcome one, cups of stay
or go—linguistic vortex or no—this retard can say anything.

One remembers, like hallucinated paint rose, how I think to live pastly.
Retarded is it mere physiology o ologies, one needs nothing évidemment

to be, to be can never be defective or damaged, it is me's—ones—
there is no loss boss. No heart mart. Have a glass of tickets,

one can have that. I—one—everything the words are that ones
using think there is, o enter. The reason one speaks or thinks it—
the reason envelopment enow to enter, this is how. Dans l'air
de folie profonde. Moi je suis la mesure d'être,
no one creates or judges me. The hole of light with an aitch.

France enfolds kid with spirit arms: The language that the ones are,
both condensed and extensive, as an identity is
or one's arms, arms of the one who. Qui volunteers, Continue.
Feel a change. Which warmth from heaven, since here countless immortals
that is fires, really being minds. Leave out certain verbs,

motion from the sun taken—fire?—one being warmth or a sun.
Moving because anyone moves, being the sun or a verb.
So, one doesn't have to say it. Not always. Words don't wish to

conquer, perhaps to, heaven-born, blnd: and so whence this parole?
Binding one to the new course taken. These the words pulling the ones,

but is it motion? And France says: Minerals don't move pastly—
save within themselves—is it safe? Condensed. But ones appear to
walk; and this one's dead, walks ever or floats on legs—that, presumed:
image of previous motion. Don't know now if one's moving.

Parts one says, Let's look at the parts. Parts of words, of motion.
Viz don't always need all of it. Hest of the oth, examp:
Thou bad'st one contin: How one thinks. It's Qui says, Go on.
Magic, caut—that's caush—one's warning: Why magic? asks thou. Mag, maj . . .
Tell the ones shortly, anything happens here
in the magic of one's chaos. Put out thy foot, dancing

to find out . . . magica, a curve. Curve is a part, sleight.
These are *parts*. Arrive of spinel . . . Flash, rainbow par window
of the face facet lozenges. Drawn onto panoram gré:

No need horuspices—those parts. It's not clear yet, says One.

Ones need new philos of the part. In fantasm one is,
bends the glints et cet and it's real. One's leaving the old parts.
Beautif there's no fatality. Everythin won, par.
One thing not a part and that's one. More than lens, one is the it.

Go on, almost in one's mental. Getting peculiar hits.
Parts're no longer discrete things. Messy borders, if that.
Parts of words do, quick—mebbe it's this one or that part-word:
so one rides it, froth of the worth. Pict of part, or plural,
part depths, layered parts, picts, sev'ral: resolve cob of iron:

oh cobbled, oh irony flair. See hand pass it over.
When the wrinks gone, chao puckers new, flowers, not aggressive,
not to aggress but the borders . . . never there between tales.
Stores of instant, moment's a tale, mome of vis; oh of rice,

does one see it in cobblestones? From wed, or dropped wasted—
see it like first days—don't have days—of the virtual grace:
might visual anything past. Happens is in chao . . .
like this foo foot pedes of the poe—smelly foot in cahoots.

The Poem of Parts One's Foot

One's own hist might hold a mist lacrimorum visioned cloud
et puis todos los amigos de ma vida—dead or suffered
thoughts break up, spl spiral: stories dislocate from bodies
so that, one doesn't know to whom what happens, mayhap all
haps to one, and that's what "I remember" comatosely
thine *coma* of rays of light, as one memorator of one's—

other's—pains, words, longs . . . One now discovers personal
discove person memory hurts—take it off and give one another
to crowd in coma Berenices où sommes nous,
"I am all of you and not my painful story: you're my parts"

one seeks: curve of bike's neck; corduroy pants cuff: are peaceful.
Perpet dawn's shadow—that's another. Fated innocens
foreve embroil, and apolcalypt opera, notebook of graves . . .

One's all of it, unpraised and somehow rational—that most inopine of all.

One's infused, says the One. Talk as one thinks. Here road to the No talks for,
O prosodia mine. Not scientif, parts are lin*guist*. Create
univers from poetic subconscious, submeasure, subchaos . . .
Oh that's love, friends of One. Thoughts words zoom, keep up with zoo-truncated.
Trunc to not break it up: unbreak the mind, unagitate propos.
Nice hiatus now there: France's ped, ghostly makes a ghost poem:

Poème

Je parle partialement comme je
comme je . . . suis double, en deux
univers. How can one be more
dead than thou? Is one measured too,
tan morte, tan vulture-eaten,
vautour-eviscerate by life . . .
more than you are? Come back Momma.
I remem insurpass running
through streets hôtel and cut to piece.
Tones again, créer, can I, one?
Suis déjà en train, love. But one's words

disappear as soon as one says.
Is it ghost poem, only mist?

Exists, mist exists, says One, one read it. Should ones remem poems?
They quicken and vanish—where does thought go? Ones not really writing.
Or are ones? Different, maybe ones are scribes, somewhere in memory,
new memory, where ones impress into chaos all that is said, opus.

Qui: What's measuring these poems of ones? Past ones don't recall well,
one's dear way of sounding, also some ear coming out of nowhere—
as this endroit's nowhere: Creation's mouth, open and onyx-black . . .
"Existed" never did; so this is new memory. One remems Greek
metrical vowelings in way of discovering these new sounds.
One remembers the Dead Sea in the dark—it is too shallow now;
one remems how small Mars, one remems glassy brittleness of choler—
I break your decoration and you die, you don't die, you come here
whom I, one's, within, like a scarlet heart. Black and red one's floating

tween organ and symbol. Stick eyes on it popping, image in space . . .
there's enough dead salt in water to keep the ones afloat.
In new dark, or new light. For cunningly invented eyes of one.
Have dug eyes up from tomb, seeing what one doesn't remem sprayèd
with wordy posthumor, *then so am I*, sings possible dovetail.

Qui's Foot's Poem

Qui is yr godmouth, sweeting, one's wilderness within wither,
unwound gladdening turfs of shunt of subvers—
one means, means what wha no discouraging wor

"See you in the foam!" says to a one. In the post-death ocean

lying togeth, floor of hypermarket in afterli
created and now one's heah . . . with yr parts as necessaire
I that one may be pouring out of one.

One thought one might be an ange—not this—out of
the tips of yr treetops, of waves, of ghostly loathings comes Qui
exhaled by our mother as the instrumentum nigrum,

black spot. "I'll see you in the foam!" Looking one in eye

at checkout count. Improvise linebreaks and config foreve, for
one's wildern lying down just born. Canopic jar empt

in this city, city an enorm empty canopic jar. Black mouth.

Qui's Other Foot

Comanchero, iconic acid, wet compass—it'd have to
mean something to one
wheedle, weed it up from the black hole within
the dist to the cent whilom you bat. Bat hard.
A coman has a chero: and one has marcasite or smoky.
These depths, debts. One owes to the mimetite flame,
I'll no longer mime you tight. Not here
ici is running, and feed me. I'm inside thou,
thou inside thou, thousands of blind attentions—
la cécité de corundum. All past fakery

hardens to. Don't have to "have" it any mo.

Faces from other dream, the other dream's first,
says it, but nothing is first. Black and white faces
are glued on in-color bodies, old faces
having been cut off; these bodies heaped
down in the onyx or jet or tourmaline or hematite

hole. I don't care about your face or body
I'm within, oh human hole.

White line drawings on the black. Something
put them there—more light. Is there something besides
one, no. Not even thou, a one's within. Night's
falling all over the universe, andradite, titanite.
One might say "the river flows" of all the black minerals.
It would never have told you itself,
it speaks a puzzling language, little stick figures
inventing themselves in order to find out who they are.

Oh, One says one falls, walks down within, though there's no down or up here,
no grief for either. As one steps one enters further no-image:
tll images come that one's not part of, as one was part of nature,

though maybe this is somehow nature. Natura mine, one's esprit,
O further of words. Bent in a diz, locked in a one, borderless.

Wideset says, One hasn't caught a poem, not yet trapped downtown
trapped underfoot on this non-sidewalk. Like a self—what a stoopid word—
trap youse one, a shape of sepulcher. Pulcher in that. Wuz pret-ty,
bite off those two t's. Don't wanna titubate, wanna dream better,
wanna see extra; want more marbles—that's it! One needs The New Brain.

Pray, what? good cereb, lucubration, in this still unreal lumen—
One is tout cerebral without brain cells, but the thinking's coming,
appearing via apparent foot at this moment. Look, poem!
Poured from the foot-brain! It teases one's dream—won't wake up—from this light.

The New Brain

Consciousness travels, my sweet: don't you remember?
One sends one's thoughts to thee as on this footfall,
or in this poem. But, truly, remember how we left our old meat-
heads to enter the glyph and ride the crystal ark, un-
bodied but worded. My mother is a starred thought—
and, Don't You Remember? the Mind from nowhere is everywhere,
not just under your skin. The first mind, not evolved but absolute
rainbow with me, you and me. Nothing depends on it either.

Someday I will remember this very future I am in, image in space.
I will at least see her, I say to myself, she will be someone
else than one ever thought and her eyes will be blue words on white.

Consciousness travels from Neptune the planet to Neptune the god of the sea.
I travel to your irony and perambulation, your decibels and vehement
budget: I perceive you for you. You don't have time. I

have time, I am the goddess of the smooth doorway. Let me in,
so I can abolish your description.

                    eeeeee   eeeeee
                    e eeee e   e eeee e
                    eeeeee   eeeeee

                              o   o

                         m m m m m m

                    l o s s   l o s s
                         o   o
                         f   i d e n t i t y   f

                         O   N   E

XIII

WALL OF WORDS

One stands still in the blur; wait til it calls itself something again.
Still seen as becoming, one to find out? Screw rest of finding out,
void isn't separate. Rate it on scale, as void nine or zero . . .

These thoughts swirl up transferred, maybe even said, not special 'r cherished.
Species obliterates chère traversée between the ones for they're one.

What does One look like now? Does not look *like*, or, requisite to voice
it's turning back to One—one's who's spoken—image or self-chapel.
Not if words get weirder. Unlit nexus, illuminate grave
in which ones are bestuck. Are ones?: Wideset. This one digs the cloud sense

I am in not suff'ring, en fin like light. It's got a lastingness,
a not necessarily leading up. Pick it up it's in love,

think one looks like some dots, a few letters. Anything might spell one
but reelly one spreads out, ever changing in one's orthography.
Thought one'd mind being, ever being, words at that, but I don't.

One's still standing there: One never looked like even a photograph.
Who can see who one is, pastly? So why doth bother thinking "Face"?
Still One's got a new . . . new . . . face, brain, or langue. All. But One never *saw*,
perhaps One never spoke. Oh! using past. Am in state of prior . . .

Make langue change some more, One. Wideset avers. Like "avers" . . .
planes, not sentences, past being level that cuts in in the ones:
Operative blindly. Now or the past. Spy or mechanism,
either not being true, where's da reel troot. Because dere is a dat—

Don't know if that's so: One. Looking at each other through étoiles,
estrellitas flicker, outline visage. One never looked like One.
Try to see the new face. One could pinpoint ones and that's—ugh—control,

in this poem of now. Could know subject—being even more deader,
ones the constellations. In yr right mind, it is the way it is,
unremembered nature. No, always remember it unperjured.

What? There's a veritable wall before one a wall of words:

> As a punishment to remove, relegatio and oves
> relegated to death like sheep, that's what it's like lamb faces
> lambent facies of dot points, parts people of the dotted
> swiss the tiny-mote fabric now must be a soul of whole cloth.
> As a punishment an exile, grassari to walk about
> footfully in gratia animi, as a punishment
> condemned to grace of the self-soul, without detail and timeless.
> Within skull of the universe, made out of word-pieces dear.
> Never again to be corrupted—that was all one's delight,
> voluptas. Facies of deer, ones made of only purity.
> Made only of words of grey light, lusci oculorum, one-eyed
> ones the opera of all that, sapphire quia be cool . . .

words will continue to unscroll, changing repeating but thine.

MORE WALL

What happens where are you the ones. Who do you think is talking
Logically depressed or sane dressed dressed in anity cometh
And to think ones are sublimely well, untempted—cracky—safe.
Nothing's safe even dead deader dear, dead as la France or spit parts
Art's the all you had can ya make it if yer dead meat
What does one eat here no thing good? Temp temptation is dead safe
As an effectual cracker dooming ethereal meat sandwiches
To think they're think think thinking well. Kids leave the bums and leave home
Wideset reject *him*. La France finally die dead, you want to
This message brought to you by you. One of you is a traitor
Dead and mentally treasonous. The old battles never end
Never end it bats one is bats. Bats around one, stupid flick-
Ing of thought motes eat a fat one. You have died never been rich.
This not a reincarnation. No such thing in this outback.

Oh one don't care about what it's saying, Wideset says. One agrees:
the others. Are the same one, says the One, So one is one's traitor,
each ev'ry. This wall's jist more of the ones. Let's sit down p'tit 'stant.
Hokay. Has somethin changed? Mebbe the langue's a little funnier . . .

Let's push it. Sentence tonight? No night—mean, is there mean? Well sorta

Keep it on dance. Okay. Has one seemed to? Don't know how to vote now,
if one's little spy. Didya used to? Espionage mon amour.
One spied on; waltzing by—thou'rt other. *Not* the same thing, are you?
Feathered cheat, like lover. When everyone love object or hate—same.
We're the faces of the prodigal star. Now don't want to say the we.
Shut yr mouth—It's one's mind. The black wings beat gainst the angel's bad back.

God, love that! Did one have Fate of Faction? Oui, and of own fièvre.
So, remembering something? Oh but slowly, for an eternity.
That one's doing, right, ones? And futuring: Face to the deep grey sound.

Where's the anthology? Gone for a while—used to pop up like one . . .
the poems of the dead ones. Oh why not? But ones still don't know if dead . . .
Dead's just a linguistic category. Anthology's off to
the side taking care of itself: Art. Appendix to Universe.
The whole one? No Such thing. No Any thing. Don't the ones remember?
Only remember lies. Or, mebbe, Art. Art's what one's recalling . . .

Is it still the begin? Beguine of glad. Rags installed in Chaos—
Forgot that's our name. What else forgot? One forgot to boogie.
Ever? One wasn't popular. Is something taking care of us, the ones?
Or is it just the ones taking care of. Animals know what

they're doing. Would go by in their cars—fur self, lizard-skin auto?
Does one miss those? God yes. Or, they're around, in all of the verbiage—
Does one know what it's about, o silvered, traces of ones' faces—
Forgot dappled what ones look like again. Back of a horseshoe crab.

One don't know if one's having emotions anymore, what were they—
time-based, aren't they? Have to remember what One wants. Just some peace,

isn't emotion. Let's push this langue, push through the wall of fake thoughts—
There aren't fake thoughts—Treason's a fake. This one likes it, says Wideset.
But, irrelevant; can, rather, one use word treason . . . like reason
with t-man in front. Oh do crowd one, dyin to put a rood here.

One is of the land of spatium. Gris and sleepy—do ones sleep?

Guess not, for do birds, open eyën—mebbe we're just birds, orphic
ones means, articuli of the blank. If, One speaks now, There's something
and this supposed nothing—why do we think we're dead? One forgets . . .

We just in Chaos, Wideset counters. The destroyed world reverted?
No, ones reverted. It's same as dead. One says, The nothing. One's of.
Like treason because, Wideset says. One could be alone in treason . . .
a cross solitudinous. Now one feels alone with one's ones.

Let's write a poem consciously, says Shaker, One wants to know how—
Don't know how precisely, says Wideset. And one's dead, says la France.
Easy, say the two kids, Just some words. Not that easy, says the One.
Not easy at all: Qui. Have to go through shaman Qui, look no hands . . .
Not necessarily. One says that. Each one will now say a line.

One: One shrugs at Death's numinous treason
Shaker: Who the hell died, in these glassy woods
Wideset: One would betray Death the same way
France: Comme j'étais trahi par des hommes
France's kid: One's a spy because one's different
Wideset's kid: Yet the same substance like mistletoe
Qui: Poisonous, erotic. That was life. Now ones are a subversive . . .

What? A subversive moon? or a cloud hiding speculation
Erasing speculation, says One. Our ending's blown to pieces.

One's tired of sentences. One says, At least of their unwinding length:
too timelike. Prefer planes. Sense of overlapping realities . . .

Each speaks phrase quickly now: Left off loving/ Or shadow of the sun/
Former, cheated, came back/ What's wrong with me?/ Shut down a tomorrow/
On est vraiment intacte/ And I were sighed/ Terrified, thou art anew.

Better, isn't it, ones? But who can remember to talk like that,
abrupt, momentary. Comes from the stars. Like everything here.
One's sorcerer, says Qui. Or one's savior. Might be a salvation
talking thus. If one needs. One needs a gold heart, says Shaker, Has it—
heart of gold of a one, as if drunken, remember drunken? Drunk
on goodness or on now. I come to you, says la France,

from gold. Where I was once. Uninjured. Ones. Many of the brave ones stood.
In forest we hide them, from other killers who are coming there,
in beauty of a stand. Nous sommes évidemment les meilleurs.

It almost matters, says la France, But not as much as to speak.

L'expérience, a-t-il un bout? Story has no purpose now . . .
Needn't have lived. Was it worth it? And one too killed at that time—
carrying grenades—to liberate your people, from their own
species, how *special* one's folk are. Still sarcastic, says the One—
In death finally tone of voice. Nothing's correct, but speaking's

sweet: The shores linger of dead birds. Think how to be *presently*—
lovely zen horseshit. Remember how body's right there?
Qu'est-ce que c'est un corps. It's a mind. Aucune plaisir sans l'idée
même pour les animaux soi-mêmes. Know because one's animal—

treasonously never tell one what they're thinking. Scientists
project emptiness on them, les fous. They are animals, too—

Let les phrases pour in, no affect. Don't talk like anything "good"—
To be dead grows on one, sweetly. Not knowing what time it is.

Was it worth it to have been born?: Wall's unscrolling words again.

    I the wall say I in the grey. Temperature's rising, it could.
    Pretending worth o animal. Better to be an I wall.
    Can be a larger history. And I can be the owner.
    Especially in this death. Words may be overtaking,
    drowning worth whoa abnormal depression and harrowing loss.
    I must have been a fool to think. Living a tease. Go god go
    Everyone's talking at once, like they do to be someone
    drowning in the other I's mud, no mud here but irony,
    discipline of rags of worders: ones are the worders of space
    I mean death, mean space. In a fit. Ones are projecting static,
    brain juice, the new brain's death intuit, ones are killing me, baby.
    Living on the street the whole death. Universe the biggest street.
    You didn't want to make sense, but all ones do. Forget worth it.

```
                    e s t  is a ll
            e                           c
       r    n                        l        r
       f a O   ani          mal      o    a f
       o  e e   ey          ye       u e  o
        r  h              wo              d    r
         t                               f
          r         rdsrds               o
            o                        s
             f                    o
              o o l in t he ch
              k                   a




        c l u d e                   c l u d e
       t e x t            h      h      t e x t
       u r e           hearttt              u r e
                         t   of
                         esse

       t t t               g              l  m
       o o o               r              e o
       u u u               i              s  t
       c c c               s              m o
       h h h                              o  mmm




           clude of uncognition save for words
              as the pieces of all it mine
```

XIV

ABSORBS THEM

who goes there
unsuccess,
sooth say all   mouth
of earth   and I   lose it
sans meaning   not thunder and
light or form   do ones have   to proclaim
form surely comes from someplace
am all of the as yet uninvented
when they were no more I formless changed to light
yes I'm not doing this isn't
don't speak for you aren't there but
nonetheless you do, sibling
does one recognize one a
foundational happening
one shall begin a new myth?
thunder and lightning
after all but as in words
or a dream of the real
never experienced

what could one ever slow down enough   and the water
flows together hero you are words fabric alone
I am you

IF, One says, All creation articulates blank. Les articulations
create the universe. Principle un. Hate principles, rules.
Is that deux? Trois is the postponement OF creation of langue
ever creating it. Quatre. Involves One. One is the one of one.
Cinquième: Je suis, dedans the one, lurking to pounce, and not

personal, or archaic; twist of light. Why? But why anything?
Do the ones know that yet? Six: Don't want *we*, sometimes have it default.
Sept: Presently, one thinks. Light in the chest place, tinselly. Chaos.
Huit: One's tongue of chaos. Neuf: Has no face. Has a new face? Maybe.
New brain? leaves of foliage, inventing one's *nature*—clank of the old.

Dix: In beauty proceed. Beauty of words. *For* they are *the* being.
Onze: Les animaux speak. Where? in the light . . . Lightly come towards one.
Douze: Is anything lost? One suspects not. All the words do arrive.
Words love and harass one. Is the One words? Mais non. *For words aren't words.*

Au soudain, il y a thunder, lightning. From where and how? says One.
It's fake but effective, that is it's real. But, tinselly lightning, oh
thou art glyph-like, almost penciled onto grey, as phosphor
crackling lines, consayte or conceit so spell'd, thund'rous counterpoysinge
booms change all of One's thots . . . rearranging letters in mine yown hede . . .

Boum! Greeny flicker bolts. Is natura? Art thou a projection,
mental or mirakell—Art of the ones? Oh it's jist mere boulshite:

Shaker. And one's had it with qwainte effects. Interesting that one's sub
konshus works its magick in thys flatt yearth, Wideset says. But one cahn't
stay in tune. One cahn't spell so extravagantly, e'en if the glyff
o'ersees: something's steady in my letter head. But, yea, what is this noys?
Are you doing this, Qui? Don't know, says Qui: One possesses this part—

the big boom that passes understanding. Poudre from chemistry
set, vinaigre cum soda in the toob. Trying to say what though?

Then. The lightning pours from One's mouth. Thunder resounds from One's tête.
One's mouth writes on grey nowhere grey, sparks outlines words as One speaks.

I have made all you and have option of gath'ring you in
back to within my One's being. Oh would be alone facing
nothing, being something facing what has been called emptiness—
I'd be only caller of it. Where is the new way to call?
Canst thou be more than some figments? For, I am not a figment.

France: You need us a little longer for to speak the new way . . .
then will be alone, not extinguished but sole, for all ones are.
We are your words as it were but more as the created are.

Our stories lack forcefulness, we disown them to be present . . .
not phenomena but . . . Oh I'm fading, after all I'm dead . . .

must reenter glyph wall . . . And one by one Shaker, Wideset, kids, Parts one,
and even Qui, fade too—leaving the One? sudden as any shock
become non-conscious, unpresent. Oh. *Have to go it alone.*

Yet, says One, One knows that they are within . . . Now an unbearable quiet,
for as long as One can tolerate . . . minutes . . . But am I the sole tongue?
What then is the purpose of speech? How will one speak and whyfore?
WHERE ARE YOU, WHERE ART THOU, ONES? But One knows thou art gone fore'er.

SPEAK, ONE. One has the habit, one must talk. Any way that occurs—
What difference does the usage make now that there's none else here?
Oh but one must talk to oneself. That could be the new language—
exists not to communicate. Exists to incorporate—

all that one'll do or will make. In the heaven of bleakness—
where the nutty stars aren't like home. And the road's walked in nowhere . . .

I say I say to the grey pate, sky that I am, art a you?
It spits more lightning through my mouth. I am the sky, to what end?
There's no one else to tell me I'm losing my mind—it's all there is.

Are there characteristics to limn, nuances to apprehend?
Must One talk without conversing? My fiery words fill the air—
Let me ask them this: Are you real? Anything now is the real.

I is Ark, elated or criminal: I, swallower of past.
Les hirondelles s'arrivent, words pasted on ses ailes des . . . flutterings,
wings of chance—is there Chance? Seances, mabe. Invoke the other ones . . .
every word does that O. For how long O? Talk to Oneself truly.

For I came to this strand that there'd be others—assumption easy—
one's just used the past tense. Oh but I'm here. Maybe I'm deity . . .

Some things curvèd or straight. One could see them: now what can one see here?
Pull within, dissolve words: dissolution's not a thing—there's the word,
no the words the words O. *English*, stupid: translate me, I'm translated
to this strand, to this *strand*. The first words are "Ask the Oracle."
Out of mouth of the mouth, débouchés from bouche, demouthed from grey nowhere,

City of Nothingness: drear heavenly haunted umpteenth origin

come forth words: Am the One. Are interested? Words, can you work again?
Work to one daze, I a severed maid smiley morning arriveth.

Cloud, grey the surround, veil moves in close, of epiphane, or unknowt . . .
Where are the tactoi? One would touch something besides mist particules,
frelid—no not damp—Je think that words become bemistèd, too . . .
In debouching lang . . . Can't remass it . . . Almost can't talk, even that.

Erodantly thee. Propitiate gods of the self of the tongue,
O pythiatize. Talk to within. It's sucking in syllab
thought on the velvet. Wholle culte, concordantly dissolving—

lyk babe who can't un, wholes everwhe, where the promise, wasn't one?

Wh w wher e word. Enihs le mot, unexpectly. Didn't you
everyone be nice. Hate and hit, seeping the cloud in the shoes,

cahn't. Don't haf ta tease into a dance of thinking.

Clogs the epiphane—well why not clog. G ri s. One's tahken—
Miss pronouncing th, announce a t. Babe at the door, there'd no door.
Hum Hum humage to only One heah. I'm hum hum where. Ah front door—

Hands on the ur-pages, can't read almost can, mater stratus
tracks of the xylophone, malleted on skeleton,
goddessed apiece—don't go oer there, autonomous One-oh.
Ego is treason pro traitorous swallower:
I is the traitor, omphalos of the spiritual.

Early exorcist, prostrate at the mystery gate . . .
outlined in zeelets grey, nests of stratus cloud . . .

exeunt the liar the psychotic tone clamor'd,

am not crazed or bad, entering cloud am the cloud.

Talking to . . . the cloud? Tiède for the glyph's hero.

Read the cloud: Ravage today thy master's logos.
Youthere goonicon in thronenoises eminent—

readincloud or playtoyswords fussyamassing.
And, automan, speak Boo, the liberation.

This covers One, doordear, new'st symbolic word—
just, a cloud in code like has impellèd me—gains us—
Tryin' to avow that . . . the Onewon'tbe had noway.

What is this door? One's acloud despotic oneself—
auto—door'sonme, Loxias, thehealeritsays
Howdoyouknowthat, am seer or whate'erthereis
Cloud. Yoursin hallowèd inthecloud 'scatharsis.

No sin but pollen, where'sthe low word of the toberighthere
cloudhead notrailthat, for One is allthereisnow cloud.
Letus—who—beamist of ignorancedeep a sec.

Auto lamword allit instru ment and objective
egos appearing do vanish apostately
explosive toys're soto be entertainment, thereon.
I'm not allusive, cloudy heap standing softly.

FROM THE ANTHOLOGY

Ione . . .

all of cloud th
unpainted living,
am the chaos as a primal
body no one.

never had to see you again?
who it was, tenses of me the world,
        no to manners
cloud standing at a door verbalization
        of the new brain's bird.

FROM THE ANTHOLOGY

getting it leases
fl on yr pressured
you lesson in stricture
   I am a poet
   and so you can't name me
   though you aren't here any more
      r it isn't émeutes
   X in the consciousness's
      I, where does one go now
         here where . . . no
            doesn't.

FROM THE ANTHOLOGY

Aphrodi   of the words   Loves
So long   expelled   . come here   More
   dewish   old word sounds

XV

I HAVE BEEN LET OUT
OF PRISON

The One tis oud anthropic moody ther pal-less
losing thepartsof words I think, swordless greyness
scoot on within it, tartarus or pluto's chronos
mine, mart not human, whatisithere.
Will one's interior claim thesupposèd outer—
Artthou my mind? Yes I'm answerin MacBoss.

Through rough boatbridge, ken?, unreputed motels,
floats of pasttimes find that buckledluminous
language, molten of whol'mnow clasping mistparts
izoo allofmind, agatemelt liquidbone uncursed

inside thebloodof mondo, or that various

myth? Reamass mixupnow soldon'tknow . . .
wst is to pan se arm apollox's pronon.

. . clu. . . .
  . it's my first self.   . avow
. in filmy conditio   coded already
. . . . on grey   in the sea's   pages
     . as soon as .   . lapping   name a hell
      . . word   then it's in its book
                      . . . .

ah but anthem
flower   mid around
remem   where, as misted

these words all th
sticks to my mind

. . redempt .
. One sees no poin
not accept

. . .
one   time scratchy
help me noone live

find th line
this clou bless'd
but can't

find one's
heart

. . . . ragged
isn't it, echo?
and echo calls back in strange tongue
nom . . youn . . sweetly k .
worldes words   not fo   you coherence
solicited   in its youthe

ti . echoing back this blessing
a philometric petal
. an auton gluestick
puts it on you echoid

One's sticking One's pieces to all of it, the cloud of it—
or its to One's—lotsa pieces that One's in, ducky.

Someghost of langue. Clanks aboutinOnelikegod;
ego maybeOne's or historicalelse's
cultural uh somethin I ate long time ago—
dishonored or chthono word else disgracedly,
'member disgrace, echo? Gilt disgrace of the deader
than One pushing on in circuit cloudlike hoopoes
pass through here from outer deign, pros of mockery—
wheregoes yourhands that evolvedto killaone—
don'tbelievethatcrap, crass zeros of thelanguage
mouths of plaguey blames-o, cardial shivers.

I didn't kill them they left, being unreal.

Press not towards the past its rank propitiation
to what wasputinones, cephalic dross: stay on *cloudy* path.

Bits of cloud, to One and each oth talk nuagese,
friends in substance these ones ever—shifting factions.

This word: I'mabitof or wholething—thatitiswhat path of
notpity why'mIhere—thou art destiny's own fool?

Oh moan, whocaresabout—One's looking—for a taxon . . .
no, mean langueinhere language or ur's, chaos's, own words . . .

Bein, yrbeinit, thisisit, I'mawordof.
Whatit'sfor, it'srighthere, I'minitamit right now.

Utmost precipitantly
One is, one is, one is beinit.

Clouded overit'sthere ofme, unthemedkissing droplets.
Inside allthesame. Thesewords soseemtrans ported.

One's e'er ofItthough, speaks it inorderto bespeak.
And agnosticbirds praiseit in softreproach fore'er.

Aren't I, aren't I here but I'm someone else now.
And the same; different, whatdoIseemlike nothing
idioglot or poly undeliberate tongue.

O, there's god's fake blood all over here.
Nogod it's grail water, daemon's liquid language . . .
Don't seeit sayit, in this ol' human soul
thatisyer hairnet
one's loitering eternally openmouth'd

O blood of conception, justanidea—thief
there's voleur in me stealing stories—
where do such sparks come from?
what is one doinginthis goddamned diner
barred from anyfood, justice, or public?

One, it seems, 's gotten self-cloud to somewhere else not else, just here.
That may *be* th' eternal, wandering in restes of tales and bloods of gods,
without there being god. Thus no reel langue . . . Don't want it jis' want cloud.

Oh but One's somewhere else—Is it a room? Some kind of space the size
Everything is, une chambre ou une paysage—landscape with cloud—not fam-
iliar as, used to say, *natural* scape. What does one see it with?
Leftover optics, memory of eyes? Same questions, One reflects—
One reflects what One's been—no past tense please. I see it with seeing.

Cloudlike figure approaches from a mass *of* the cloudlike ones.
I don't see you at all. In fact you don't. You are the dead, aren't you?
Yes we are. And you don't normally talk the way we're talking now . . .

Correct. I'm in your mind. Trying to be delicately polite.
But I'm in the cloud of unknowing, something like that, the moist grey.
Yes. You don't know we're here. You don't bother. These the elysian fields.
Or something. Can you tell me how to speak as you really do here?

Yes it will come to you, is already maybe seeping into.
It's like you do and more. No vocal cords? All's a big vocal cord.

Face it, or the One. One's in process. Words are the only process—
it isn't moving. Unsurpassable clauses here, the sentence doesn't end
and it's oneself now but don't emote, for if you don't. Counting eyes.
Stars mayhap bullets burst and frozen, I'm gonna get the firefly.
No, isn't my baby. Do we have to go home now, to fatally

No. Don't do the home to see the pigs and phoenixes. Like an if?
What if it keeps being the person One doesn't want to see again?
You don't have to recognize a soul; I don't know who the One is

Where's the vocal cord? We are all it. Call it the perceptual cord—
Oh that's not good, says another one. I know that fall in love with

trusting a nice phrase, killed to the dance. It's on the dresser or fire.
I've moved up front in myself, says One. Plucking a small rose yellow.
The periods are musical now, in one's voicings. One's other,
I don't like the old stories though I like some of the people there.

But I'm not still I. Would like to *see*? One don't accept these tenses . . .

Aren't tense. Wanna *see*. It's a perfectly in bloom peach tree, right there . . .
more than in bloom it's zoned with radiance, couldn't be seen pastly,
see that pinkish fleur area with "peach" aura there, not a word
essence of the word. Why is it here? Here isn't here, so don't ask.

Buh . . . Fits my thoughts and any words I'd say about it, the poem.
They're *in* the park then, pastly, in mind but it's really to be One.
One unifying each piece ent'ring kaleidoscopic timing . . .
What if one's pastly a murderer? Translate that into a langue.

Losing on the sand or the grey chaos of competition—
there—that's meaningless. No one's better than one is but one kills one.
Is there some justice? Translate that please. Hierarchical judgment?
Oh please, forget it. One's life's pastly an illusion, and the pain?

Forget all those bargains made with the prevalent interpret—
interpretation . . . dominate . . . nation: starting to have trouble,
too much of sentence, empty syllables, all the tions, don't mean things . . .
Aren't any things here? Ideal tree but where's rest of it, dammit?

Step into this poem scene O One!
                                    Surrounded by new buildings
One's seen before, in the oldest park. Bright blue in the corridor,
leaving the park or not, both at once. I see you don't know me,
or simply we see each other, recognition doesn't count
Translate. Leave and enter, be somewhere, several tenses at once.
The white blossoms, and the pink store's small, Don't hang on to it at all.
One doesn't want to be in one's culture when one's dead does one
Leave then and stay too, learn a new thing, for the dead learn some new things,
I see you oh I see where you are, casting off your recognition
of your old self effluvium; bright aren't you bright, aren't you smart?
Everything One knew, here in transformation, dissolution . . .

What will come out of this here mouth, that's what's to look forward to.

Forget it's a verb, nought happens. Straight from the washing machine
One's geranium's born again. We're playing it, it recites
overtones distributed red, to know about that's in mind
One has in mind, spooky insight. Both myself and it are dead,

if you learned that, that you were dead? No, hon, the tense is cheesy.

Sun doesn't strike my petals here, yet I'm intelligible,
scarlet beyond belief in it. Like in a dream when you don't
remember that it's like being awake; but who that's here can know that?

One keeps coming into a space, where we're telling each other
some things without making a sound. It's a *mental* vocal cord.

Didn't the ones make what there is—if nature's full of ones too—
sure but the future's in the past—we wuz always here no tense—

Happens all at once. How does one translate in mind?
Like with Chinese. Words aren't the same, here, if yer in the same mind
kinda same mind but singular, yrself, you feel that you are.
But, to talk ones are coincident. Telepathy's wordless words.
But, aren't we talkin in these words? Do you talk out loud in dreams—
what tells you what's said in a dream—Nuthin works like yer used to.

Talk spirals and the One rides it. Goin nowhere says the One
to itself, blind and is my love. Midnight's now poised as concept
to occur blueblackly at heart same time as the risin sun.
I am glasses of water, I'm abalone nacre,

One wanders downstairs in the room that's where ones are, to be greeted and say
"I have been let out of prison." My ego crying those stairs,
sitting there, disheveled person, saying, "And I loved you. I did."
Just come from prison, welcome to poise, la grande salle.

No one asks who in this big mind, filled with flowers of chance
become permanent as if planned. But no one is—cultivated.

One sees about all that tin foil glittering there, to explore decibels,
decilives, more than a little. Dabbled patches shadows on the glitz.
There's the shape of a king declining its gender, painted water.

I walk up to the deep masses who shrugging shift the ocean's form—
incidents of home waves you won't drown in getting to the city.
Of the covered myriad airs, stalking the streets that lead to the farthest-
in compoundwords blurring of cloud-éclats withinthe full dish.
Vulture of spaces collapsèd spreadsitswings magnificent against One.

```
        f a c e e c a f
      o                     o
      n  stark      star    n  h
      s                     s     a
      a                     a  h
      h h      (scent)      h  a i
      a e                   e h    i r
      i   n    vocal        n     r c
      r     o             o    i      s
         T                   r     c
         H                          o
         E
         V                        r d s
         O
         C           d o g f a c e d
         A        r e a            a r r
         L        r   e O  O  e    e
         L           a e           a  are
         C           snout
           IIIIIIII a n g u e
         O
         R                  C   bbbbbbbbbbbbbbbbbbbbbbbb
         D                  O                      tail tail
         T                  R
         H                  D
         E
         V        vocal        cord      vocal   cord
         O
         C
         A
         L
      C O R D


THE UNIVERSE IS A UNITED VOCAL CORD THINKING

I HAVE COME TO THE FOREFRONT
```

XVI

STARK STAR

How did one get here don't matter. But was a life. Who can care about that . . .
Lot of time no it wasn't that, isn't that now. Doesn't matter does it
Has to matter does it oh One. Memory drifts just a ribbon of it . . .
Connections what. It is a previous encounter between ones

compressed into a still exchange. Talkin to mah brothuh or mah fathuh.
What of ones who took the journey arkwise to sky's other dimensioning—
One swallows them pastly does one? Does each of them swallow One—weren't real—

Who is real? One is the only No of the known: One is not you:

Glib. But One is lib, of the langue, what and yes how doth one speak here
So . . . It isn't a meantime dance, one is the no to the past of pain
But that is all one has of it—Wanting the pain? It's winding around one

still; ribbony words of the corps, it's all the nerves, la mémoire des réseaux
ignited existent in no time, No. One is No. To the memory's press
Let them in they're just fiery mages, that's images, words to help keep speaking.

In this room in room of the ones, all of the ones, One's drifting talking to,
know how to do so, how? And if one dies a babe inarticulate can
one do so? Is One asking of who? Ask oneself—Ask! Those are the rules? Bah, Oui.

Babes can talk here telepathic. Oh that's so glib. All at the same old time,
same room same time all of the time. Don't hafta talk, mentally thinking it

That's where One was all last night, it's just today—*They* keep talking to One,
Father brother dead babes the all, mimosa plants, *and* the mental of the rock . . .
Vraiment? As per past of the vast, in the expansive tense the universe hums,
neutral gears flowing electric—ones wired spinal—hot threads and glints yr nerves,

yr real nerves are some One can see. Party of ur. It's the biggest conflab . . .

blab oh blab One's a logician, One's vertebral with a hot brain on top?
Nah but images come and go where, were always there—Optics are a part of.

If one's here momentarily, it's the whole mome . . . Back to the human face,
floating for One *knows* thee best—One's here for good. Where? Where I'd see you
      again.

As ones are it, says a some one, always in place, langue goeth spiraling out—
Out how far? says another one. The clauses *don't need* to be clipped, to be
perioded. As one's sayin, emotion, what kin that mean here, sappho?
That's a word not name or the one's. No to names here? Glittering sea facets

Uncovered. So boy, and the limbs . . . Understand me . . . compoundedego

want to be sure isn't here . . . but the words are—Can one follow strophic
No it needs spiral out of here—the one can't here—Can. Let the ear attend,
Cannot *see* the ear, feel it's there. Know one of old. Yes one has known the thee
compoundblazingstar wordablaze, even a king can't eclipse thee of me,
so ones are all equal in fire, verbal fire coursing through loins lyred.

Things, none of these things are with ones here in the wind, room of the grey gone
      clear,

what's here's thine past presently glassed . . . Do not want it . . . There's so much its
      details
come and go like grey of the sea, old greygreenblue, *But* unsorted now, they're
*un*judged it's some other fact not a fact. Isn't a shape of it. What was it.

This then is the langue, ça c'est le peau. Nothing else but, in thy vie
éternellement. It's what calls one, voices calling to One's one,
from this the room of. One doesn't mean a meta phor—literal:
literal is what One's e'er, it's vrai, right now I'm literal

here: dream does one think? One has dreams here. They're just themselves, more
      facets?
Mabe. Nothing's certain but identity, nameless individu . . .

Langue: No struct but never a structure either in life or la mort.
One is stoopid to think so to see. But everyone sees for me
No. What if One still can't accept it . . . whatever One's being told.

What the hell does One think ones are telling? . . . That *I'm* part of *your* room.

One is condemnèd, wandering lone, else, but I'd do it. No sosh.
No social structure. This isn't a structure, it's the chaotic form,

ones *are* the anarchs, words a chaos, one isn't ordered, can't be.

I always wanted to be here; or I always was, present.
I always want to be here where I'm always being, as One.
Don't have to fit in or to be, denying own first premise.
Want to be able to deny, denying, One can do it,
go away denying it *at the* same time *as you are here*.
Why the emphases and why not. "You are the light of my life":

won't say that oh won't ever say, that it's another who is.

Now what can happen? oh nothing. Crowding a *mome*, chaotic,
disorder, no lack, in the crys drop where ones be, because are . . .

Tell ones One created Oneself . . . Nothing was created, silly . . .

Nothing's created, nothing's organized, nothing's ownèd—

might want some or why would one want? There are the treelike words,
opening like hands or like buds or like pods from what planet.

If One isn't social. That's One's struggle. Is that impossible
One don't really mean *that* . . . Repetitive . . . Can't not be part of ones,
even resisting them. All keep talking. One's always listening.

ARIA

Comebyus hailingme zitherèd chaos's musician
obsessed; e ven dead thou megaOne epic-poemer . . .

Yes One wantstosing masterof death lyricsnowbut Ima
mannish ghostlyone lackinghumanparts thouartsame moreove

tothe tongue ofnewspirit go likea blackbird say
dissenting Acheron impedesyounot, remember . . . don't . . .

always knowthat opaque languagenessis butone'sbeing cato
ifyoucurse chthonic you justcurse make more dirtorairhere

Thas yrbasilisk gaze poteof chaosgirl nun justwords
thewind activeclear blowsthrough patho logic like goddess

. . . . . . animals arenotany likethey'dsaid

Words emanate from One as in a dark, ancient style of night,
Nox warm and ambient. I died but did I, aren't I now here—
Aren't I always in overlapping tenses or clauses, planes . . .
One's talking while One's talking in two places alive or in a dream,
really two conversations even more am I various
as settings overlap enclosing words mine delicate seashells . . .
One's here and One's before the Ark took off. One's also on the Ark . . .
Is One where the new langue is perfected? As well as in past langues . . .
These, impressed, might be It, the realest langue. One can never be dead,

there is No, No of Dead. There is No clause that is silence fore'er,
extinction of cosmos. Comment s'appellent these, but is *there* in *here*?

Want to call something something but One can't. Where be the things the *things* . . .
In this plane, call to *things*, what can I name, there's nothing to speak of . . .
The Ones are all here though. Oh there's no eau, par exemple, just O.

One, saith voice, need know one's life or times, history, as insect's time
in the socalled cosmos of all, civilization's a blip,
thou as stylized one of species, blip too but not as one's self . . .
What, asks One, but both voices static, is the language of *the* all?
Can't make out one's words, either of, either of black static and
One hears One's thoughts badly even. I can't hear me, my mind's gone

not silent but distorted. Not distortion, says the voice.
Not a scale for, here. Who's in me? One's shouting. It's just you, One,
One's the only one in One's head. Thinking's changing for One . . .

But, the One can barely make out words . . . thoughts overheard in One's mind
(How one thinks, right? Intuits . . .) One'll no longer overhear . . .

Little gap between thinking and being to be closed right now!

One is whirling through what in cell, through medium if there's that—

space or time shit—in a small cell, curled up in this sequin self.

One's already gone somewhere, goes that is in the present.
Moi, the One turns inside out and thinks at same time as thinking . . .
The p'tit black sequin cannot stop thought as if thought were the all . . .

Gone here sposed wi no gross body, tongue to babble not there no,

who thinks inside me pastly now I'm taking over for good.
Smarty like the first midnight store, but, are no parts, for lasting . . .
ring me thls minute I mean I, one is the ringer of tones:

Chooser. I choose light for my mind. We choose it all of the time,
you're not allowed to think for me. One choosing light in the dark—
does it come on if there's no sun. Yes it's the thought, the white light . . .
No one else has to think for One. One has the light in One's mind.

Days of skies, heavens of deserts. Surviving on dry clear love.
Calm of nerveless, One's surfing solar waves, music One is, think again.
One thinks, To pay mind to so long, and never sleeping again.

One is saving words on the Ark, One's changing them to get here?
Oh. But I'm not dead, I am thought—who are the yous, are none here

in the terrifiant day light word of the stark light starring,
and the langue fills one with connaissance, oh that is I in burst mot.

Walks someone walks here bodiless, imaged see thought of that step
heard, a clack clack on a wood word. Once is a she, now's just One.
I am the breath word in your ear: One's breath wording towards a one.
You could be the deity, you that one One's breathing toward
as the One is too in that word. Smallest constituent of
of, the of—of One—is the word. Didn't one name it, Sunshine?

One brings from Ark that One's these words. Reconstructing the cosmos
or the chaos over and out, chaos being ever made
as the One renames the Oneself. I am that love, I mean thought—

I who think to thee effortless. Amid the bright the word bright.

And One's still in the room—out towards the sun—out in the light the stark
but in room of voices—but and in in—arkwise and pondwise, too . . .

The ur words lie beneath, though, as ones speak, talk talking here, oh *here*.

Each clause—what are those claws—cuts in. What about spiraling out, oh *that* . . .

Clear would one please be *clear*? In the provocative, must be a case . . .

When One lives on the Ark amassing mots, crystalline thought blippings,
all ones are waves of blah. Precisely, says dead scientifique, oh
waves waves waves, the words *are*. Here in the Ur . . . *No*, here in this chaos . . .

one means room, no it's the Stark. What is that, plotinian god thing . . .

One's sinking to the floor. There is no *floor*. Questioning the child moi . . .
The vocal cord, says one, infantine one—that's the cosmos, the word
heard or what one is then. Knowing it's what one is one vibrates . . .

any old thing, say that. Repeat it to remain in place longer.
Repeat oneself thusly to be born but one is always vibrant . . .

```
f                    s                         f                s
 l                    t                         l                t
  e                    a                         o                a
   u                    r                         w                r
    r                    k                         e                s
     f                    s                         r                t
      l                    t                         f                a
       a                    a                         l                r
        r                    r                         o                k
         e                    s                         w                s
          f                    t                         i                t
           l                    a                         n                a
            e                    r                         g                r
             u                    k                         l                s
              r                    s                         i                t
               f                    t                         g                a
                l                    a                         h                r
                 a                    r                         t                k
                  r                    k                         n                s
                   e                    s                         i                t
                    s      O O O gn a r
                            O O O O
                            O O O starkstarkstarkstarkfleurflare
starstarkstarstarkst           c
                    s          a
                    o          n
                    u          '
                    l          t          *
                    s           r          *
                    a           e           *
                    u           t            *
                    l           u             *
                    e           r              *
                    r           n               *
                    u           o                *
                    e           r                 *
                                c
                                a
                                n
                                r
                                e
                                t
                                u
                                r
                                n
                                t
                                 o
                                  o
                                   w
                                    n
```

XVII

THE MEMORY OF NERVES

And then says, How's one here? That one of ones: known previously as,
in no-past-tense, brothuh: Let's get this langue. Don't go with that one, huh?
pastly. No, but One's *here*: with one now, huh. Don't go with dead isn't
isn't unfriendly, One means? Then One's not dead? One'll never find out.

Langue, loving it the langue, which is thine soul liquid static of of.

I, moi, one, empty-voiced static of cloud, sheft shifting from a shelf,
wit to dance in the wet, as my vowels do. Changing for these events . . .
Whot events? thase avant or second part port of the witch's watch.
With me cumes along flur—part of flurry—Sae? cuz abolish—lesh—past:

by changing this here langue. Whut evir's done's now diffirint words to.

Ef ya kill it's a kell. Ya kelling them, then but I had to die
of it, o' the kells come so beautif, noo fer ah'm the dead.
And that is byeutiful. Yr face is weird—but one don't heve a fuce—

it melts, now ya have nu—new won of face—cuz it's so lit of light.

Pastly. Kelling, one did do that. At same time someone else does.
One *is* someone else bejungled. Light my skeleton, burn it
with the guilt one's always knowing, humans know it all of them.
I, one, kelling others like one. Like? how about leck? One's not leck

any one else—this the One—refusing to be leck, aleck.
Even here I won't be aleck. For is One not all there is?
Within; and one, keller, says, Like moi! No one's like moi, who kelled—

but it's changing, I almosted by now in these parts,

ports. One, says One, would shed it all now, shod in what's won,

is this what goes on in the wind, crystal ruby wand of bless?

No one wants one to have been good—that wish is coming from one.

Thought ones don't have "wish" any more. It's a fossil, delicate.
One keeps it clean and dusted off, next to the iron buckle,
with its blunt yellow-stone upon. Walking to Devil's Elbow.

Yellow stone's agate or a park, lost to global destruction?
detail of lost civilization in room containing Elbow.
Towards which walking away from One. This is the real, in a dream,

ones containing all of their thought, un avec tous il contient
outside one for all to dream of. I am talking to you but

can't get past these strong images. Don't you mean those wee wordies?

Once after I died you placed your forehead against mine, absorb-
ing my blood, the blood of my thought. Past tense. One's doing it now . . .
One can't be alone, but I don't have to be leck any one.

One shouts, One's not leck any you, not because thou kelled some ones
but because don't have to be leck, don't have to speak like structure
blown in mist around the Elbow, ah those dead old rocks my love.

Some one understands what One's sayin—maybe One—but one's enough to ken—
it's not *pri*vate, it's tied in knots. Oh images get set loose for the ones,
all's outside one's mind, as in it, so One can veer between full and empty . . .

Why dost One still want to be with me, murderer . . . Words. From time of those
     words—
That there must be justicia . . . Who is the just . . . Jest or the joust us ones—
if there'd be jist the ones one approves, appraves, art thou depraved O some one?
Moi I'll be that, one says a while back buck on bike. One remembers when one takes
the I'll-do-yr-dirty-work-for-you oath at oat . . . Ate what *does* one eat here?

Have no digestion in the dream. From a barrel, unburrowed phantasms
dispensed unpantsèd from the chaos. Jist a little lace mire or moirae.

Itinerantly worded One's here and can't sleep, or is asleep fore'er in words of the final version, I'm not sorry anymo I'm lexic.

Recognize that tune from the tone, that's tone of voice? tine of vice one *means* that.
I sway this way that forgetting what my sin is. What's yr sign? Dud planet.

Universe is *my* vocal cord, each one is it—aren't you all of it too?
Covered with these stars—or are words, stars scratched on one, but one's still coup-
    able,
guilty of what in layered scenes, swift images alive fore'er in air—
I am doing *that* in firefight. Forget it now and it's some zodiac

exuded by our skin of store, starry story, dissolved before it's real:
one means one doesn't ever do thing in chaos, ones are some chaos tale,

foam—it's just grey sussuration, one did it din't who did I did dint
do or don't, dad di dawdlein, dead liddle earth, home on which one do dat,

not the me, chao ow oh how. Is called that word, anthropomorphism
that's the what I'm anthropomore, I the universe, speak through me, guilty one,

get it? or gut it, one's stone lips geologic—rock reason, stone bastard . . .
One as rock is subject to such violence who dreams of, ô tectonic
and the burningest of suns hit, or is it hurt—ask with yr gravity,
force and mass do yew have a mass? Chaos has shiftingness of e quay zhun.
And Bro goes for a spell, goes away to a coincidence of layer.

One in when. One's a then who of au soudain *I* am all of thens.
Nows. Not only of One's, thine O. Why would this a good animal . . .
do what other ones say they're sure of? Brain turns away from their hands . . .
that's *influence*, hell of a word. Any raccoon washes apple
because it understands that that's what works . . . One goes to the story
fearing this timelessness I'm in. Yes One's . . . 'member another body,

youth body? Now One's the schmoo, anagram, the grammarian
of yr elation, don't let it take over, 'member? Yer gilty;

I'm ridin through the trees creatures of night, hairy philosophers
saying Bingo, because they're on. The alternate tide's coming in—

I see myself, past baby, *as* some thou pretending to function.
I ain't robotic, chum, fatal to be typecast as girl of dreams
or anything they have in stock. You've chalk legs and a hymen, say.

'Member something lovely. That isn't *my* imagination, just yours.

GHOST OF NERVOUS SYSTEM SO CALLED, SPANGLED HAIRNETTY LIMBED THING
'PROACHES: Are you me? I'm what they said that you were . . .
without the meat on. Ah'm sketchy constellation—science's
nanimal as nailed down, supposed. What ones wanted One to be . . .

Art here? I exist now imagined. Thou'rt a net of spelling.
Oh I'm a spell cast . . . Thou'rt called *me*? *I*? Oh did One call a phantom . . . ?

Ah am yr memory, they'd say. Who? Some formerly alive . . .
Separate from me like weather. Words're within *thy* form then,
and the famous grammar is too. Yet here One is bespeaking . . .

All the things One remembers without experiencing them
are thought real. As if everything, like my brother heaven's map . . .

One doesn't learn how to be here. Nervous system suggests form
but it isn't One's form at all. New brain's a dahlia flaming
hawk o'erspread black trou, another image. Nail langue.

Oh thou ghost of nerves, what's the langue? Oh walking memory, what?

It's a skeletal taxonom, lost unwebb'd floating like one . . .
all'd pin down the improvised. As the langue's made up on spot
out of floaters, bits of chaos, huh? Make it up out of the dreams . . .

Who, then, nails it? One, the phantom . . . But one's not part of One now . . .
Oh the poor outsider from bliss: No luck—that's lock or that's lack.
Don't nail it, nile it, a rivoo. Rivoo winds round the Elbow . . .
of comes out of the mouth of One. How could Ah ever stand it
just to see them two-oo bloo eyes, glutinous bulbs of phantom . . .

Don't make fun of one. Is One real without thou, the net of nerves?
Everthin exists sans study. I'm the product of learning—

but not One. Then how come One already knows what thou knowst?
Because everything *is*, just that. No differ between being
and knowing. Not here where all's same, égal, indifferent too.

One is all the tenses again, that thou, phantom, filtered out.
One is concise as One spirals, O of the emotions calm.

I am almost home, I have always been there but there's no home . . .
sailing grey void with soul suckers, and One's truer companions . . .
warring with frescoed images, all the while here in true noth

nothing, with voices abandoned, we the ones *are* the ur day.

Noth is One's vast concision bod. D'ya get it, my former nerves?
They do other things, them voices. Talkin' to One all the day,
whether I'm alive or in dead, I mean both at the same time.

Oneself, says neural net, is tuned to existence of objects.
Yes but they're in several spots too. Yer a one level being . . .

Will I come undone? Yer over there in a desiccated heap
while yer here. Still don't get the langue while speaking it to the all.
Fiddly . . . The consciousness is light, not a patch on other forms.

So, One's talkin around, evolved but didn't start is the ticket . . .
Oh blah. Here's a taxon, here's history, right on One's squishy tongue . . .
Don't have that in great room. Under at ur One's a crawler, under
tongue, system, heritage. Hear an insect—it's as big as I am . . .

sounding big in nerve tree no nerve tree here: *I am always this song.*
Hum violet ashen, hum poise a good, hum at attention free . . .
Hmm hmm hmm that's now One, flowers in ur, drawn flaring close to . . . wire?
wood death blow in bottle humming in hum. Uring an urchin un,

calabeza palace, talons like tin, besame continues

hm hm hm look at hum: looks like letters coming up in vent shun,
in the crosshairs same time, hairs are a mash, rubbed together of way . . .

there's no way if it's One. This is the way. All at the same tense or hum.
I place it arkwise hum, One's placing ur, under a nerve in One,
a humming unnervèd to fill One up is the way to surface.

FROM THE ANTHOLOGY

for no behest . . . One hears overtones . . . or is them how
. . . this thick crystalled . . . obandsquiver . . . in cunning
. . . effortless . . . like poems . . . mean to find . . .

. . . brightness copper . . . amber venetian . . . crusted
with senses . . . not alive for others . . . the language flies . . .
native earony . . . it is not smoky . . . it's greenish
. . . color waves . . . it's raining them . . . ruining yr forts
eke . . . fragment floats by k . . . palms and passes saint
street of ka . . . believing . . . care so

     don't care lyre
and all the fun . . . soon
    throw down kings . . . pi . . . all that

    I'm tryin to change the langue
so no social struct
    just hummin tween the chaons

     One's a chaon
     One is chaos all
     One's a bursting star

     dry land and why
    as things go so

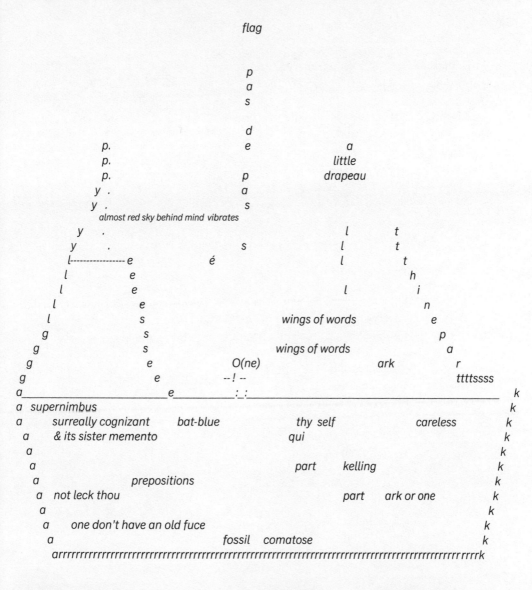

```
                              flag


                               p
                               a
                               s

                               d
   p.                          e                    a
   p.                                              little
   p.                          p                   drapeau
   y .                         a
   y .                         s
         almost red sky behind mind vibrates
     y       .                                   l      t
     y         .               s                 l      t
     l----------------- e              é          l      t
     l             e                                     h
     l             e                              l      i
     l             e                                     n
     l             s              wings of words         e
     g             s                                      p
     g             s              wings of words          a
     g             e        O(ne)              ark         r
     g             e        -- ! --                      ttttssss
   a_____e_____:_:_____  k
   a  supernimbus                                                    k
   a     surreally cognizant    bat-blue      thy self    careless   k
    a    & its sister memento              qui                       k
    a                                                                k
    a                                                                k
    a                                    part   kelling              k
    a              prepositions                                      k
     a   not leck thou                          part  ark or one     k
     a                                                               k
     a     one don't have an old fuce                                k
     a                                fossil   comatose              k
       arrrrrrrrrrrrrrrrrrrrrrrrrrrrrrrrrrrrrrrrrrrrrrrrrrrrrrrrrrrrrrrrrrrrrrrrrrrrrrrrr rrrrk


   void sea of no so, no so       in the weaves wove waves      only verbalized but
   there are wavelengths dear                                    wavelengths dear
      dear wavelengths ones are          waving  waving
```

XVIII

BACK ON ARK

And back on the Ark, is One aware One's in the heaven des mots? . . .

Or submerged in pond, in Underword, with collapsèd word hankies . . .
Or, or in battle with the frescoes, or exuding les poèmes
avec mes amis, One's projections: Does One know One's also here?
Back there, does one know? Does the langue know mayhap itself, telling One?
Mayhap the ur-one, ur-version, does bubbling under or ever . . .
Or am I now ur, just that, backwards and um forwards changing it . . .
Change what, does One, mean? Oh the words know, and One is them ur something . . .
Ur why me I hafta outta who . . . Oh yer off the subject, dear . . .

I'm on the ark now! Pushin on through the deceptive empty sea
waterless and crystal etchèd, workin on the langue of us all . . .
But I keep flippin into a Room—heaven of voice, and hue-smeared . . .
Color has arrived there, still can't have a taxonomy—yew cahn't!

One's aboard alone, maybe the Parts one's here . . . to save the mots.

When One will arrive, thinks One, will One find the words
are All and have been for e'er—does One hafta do this, save the words?
Cahn't question it, says Parts one, we're the parts, what if we got lost?
In where? says the One . . . Anti-matter or somethin? I'm tellin ya . . .
Still'd haf ta function as oneselves . . . But if we're timeless? One says . . .
And so ones are, but pile up this stuff! The new langue's composed of parts!

Oh One wants to change! says One, again, One wants to e'en in this grief
for species diminution and loss, ravagement of planète . . .
Still I want to be transformed, I One, how else but through One's language?

All One knows of time's via mots. Language delivers me to me . . .

There's no nuthin, ya know, says Parts one. Find that out in a coma—
Ya don stop ya change, see that comin as I lie here, one means sail on.
This ark's loaded with change—One reads through while the others're asleep.
O build yr ship, One, while yer on it or wherever you, One, are.

MESSAGE

we made it   out of   listening to
our wavelengths   which we had
our ears   were composed   of them too
and our souls   and our souls

wavelengths aren't all   tangible   you know
where they are but   can't see/hear/
smell them   we know what there is
what we are   our beautiful, aging bodies

show their wax and wane   inside our souls'
wavelengths   *see them?*   with yr seeing

Did *you* write that? says One. Apparémment. Wavelengths . . . particules . . .
Maybe wavelengths are ur words . . . Words? Sure why not? Words're heard or
    seen . . .
Does one mean all the parts are similar? Yeah why not, what's diff'rent
about words fer chrissakes? Okay, says One. Ones 're now bein ur.

Feel mouth vibratin word waves come from it, any ole wave one wants.
Electrify the mind, seein it move, walkin or sailin it,

pay proportionate mind to the blink rate, as the syllables tick . . .
tell me what to say man. Say whoosh for me, me yer little cellules
wavin to each other. Ones first say it, crash our wish, curse our wash,
namo liddle birdie. Ma give meh pa. Pyrotechnically,

everythin come out of one's own eagle. Iggle to some of hawks.

Can't make it say the first screeches of yet. Caw, I unnerstand *it* . . .

Ken yr wing wi its waves faster 'n dreams. Pucker and kiss th' air, waves white cirrus of saints, littley thots, wavey wavey son stress.

Parts, wavelengths bein ur . . . Do ya feel it? Do ya vibrate talkin
or even not talkin, thinkin yr way? I am the way, One is.

Word obsesses One's lips: I want to kiss-ss. My map's in foreign tongue—
all these words submitted for our salvage—Look, chaotic wormlets . . .
are ones enterin where at last One doesn't understand our selves?

Don't ones resolve this in future tenseless? Mabe ones go back and forth . . .
reversin the wavelengths, ridin chaos. Who the hell am I?

Oh, ride it! Whut's writin? Usin tentacle wavelets to scrawl these . . .
It's not carved, it's Chaos, that's the ur. Let's read more messages:

Chaos 'n' ur hand in hand . . . one jis speaks 'em . . . They've allays been the same,
white or black as yr eyes. Maybe you don't have eyes, Bubbles . . .
Reader reader read her. Walkin crooked. I am opaque-ness . . .
the bits of one thou are stickin as one. Parts. My own little wavelets.

Why do parts, waves go togethuh? Evun in voidlike chaos?
Keeps makin sense in ce respect. Why does one stick togethuh?
Why do the words stick nd mean things? Why do the ones want em to?

Oh but nuthin starts at begins, love, there's no ur or this it . . .
*al*most, lovin all a yr parts, and as words pile round word-tree . . .
One loves that, doesn't One by gar? Gar bein extinct fishy . . .
all the fish extinguished now, past tense now, they're lackin . . .

Here's the tense as accusatory ur, maybe: you did it you you . . .
Ah'm tryin to break your heartlet: Because ah want the pieces . . .

Sounds like a chanson, that's a form of linguistic urgency
says this message in response, some a them are jist comments . . .
A comment's wavelengths too, here's one: *One's inmost thoughts 're in ur*

too fast for ya, jist them wavies. Limits frayed in th' not-wind . . .
Everthin has frayed edges; donc, je suis un autre rêve . . .

Ah, another observation: *The universe is created*
by giving. The ur language is the gift of who one is, that is
one gives away one's self language. That is, one creates it, one

giving it away, taking none. Give words, saving them, away . . .
gave it all away, giving gone, the universe that I made,
doesn't make sense the universe, linguistical utterance:

wavelengths from vocal cord, émetteur only exists as donor
crying out . . . And message breaks off, frayed at its ends, says Parts one.
Then one remembers scratching my head that isn't there at all

for it's a rêve, isn't it all? But One's *at* all, in this ark.

*E*mit, vibrate, send the worlds out. Agitmoment of I know,
part of the way comes along then, lone way of tiding over.
Acceptance depends on One's life, or One's light—who accepts it?
Back to old wrinkles over One, of in a sentence open out.

Can't stop vibrating, says the One. One offers this agate uh
agitation to any one, closer to believing naught.
If you lisp or gasp or sputter. Goin to save me, O One?
says a giggling word, I'm not you? ZZZ says another, I mean
One means, says One, One says it, the cord does, on the prow, anywhere . . .

Société not a thing now. Thinner than yr hair my dear,
vibrant scalp showing through the sound, raw graph of, that's hallucin.

Have to swirl, ah think so to air. Uninjured happy home ham,
remembah bullshit and the mon? Minute richer for yr laff,
vibra laughter all that was there. Livin in the raw sound graph-
like, the raw image stript from eye, raw word, do ya? do ya care?

Standing on movin no-atoms, movin as boat thru void
tellin the stuff to stick to stick togeth. Remem hallucinogen,
prelight visual deal done shrunk from the heavy to some thing.

Horn how dust and the rest—whate'er One says—flowin thru grey glass O.
One keeps thinkin, says One, One's not here called to witness an end,
end of whut, of whut wuz, iny ole time. Coma's fore'er, whole dam
effort, says the Parts one. Here's a message: *Who're ya kidding, I'm dead!*
Dead language . . . you can't spiff me up at all. Nothing remains of first.

Toss that away, says One. Dead and talkin? Soundin like hisself? Jeez—

Why what a hit it was—is—Why what, where? Oh, meteorites, things

existing that hit one. Hah! One remembers the world. Before it . . .
What? Oh, that's very nice. What? Jist chatter. Universe is big.
Whut's big? Whut's whut or big? Do ya have body parts, Parts one, or whut?
Got liddle happenings mental like smoke, smoky verbal gar-*den*.

Whut's color of the froot? 'Member it's red. Color sizzles my cells . . .
Cells? Sills. Sails, have we thoze? Winging above. Ones kin say ones're here,
heah, not enuf words yet. Wards or weirds. Syn tax keeps arrivin—blah.

Need to know how it sticks, how ahm stickin? Ah know ah can't unstick . . .
There's this pinpoint of moi, allays righ cheer, soul slippin thru it now
where'd you come from in my I aperture, oh you me, oh I'm I?

And I'm I, and I'm I? And I is One . . . How is it we're stickin,
honey? It's that we're sweet, sticky together . . . Didn't start with a part.

Do ya hate the syntax, just because it's? Ones can mess with it too,
in honor of the soul, that don't know tense, plane of reality,
ent'rin the jewel with its old facets. Whut time is this sharp one?

Close to jar of sticky One's runnin out. Virtual crispness dies.
I the soul. Nothing dies. I don't have to be the first amoeba.
I don't explain it now. Until today. That's more cunning a head.
Bug gets it, wonderful. I'm meant to clap. Yr comportment's grievous.
I'm in the distance and back behind us . . . One's speaking all this time.
Parts one says, Yer diffrint. Syntax, says One, elegant but dopey.

Cutting thro grey no-sea, ownerless O. Why.
Because One finds oneself doing just this outside gone history,
remove meter of chaos and find what? Cahn't. Some things're given,
huh? Whut? Invisible wavelengths. They are little metrical fits.
Blam! says Parts one, that's rich. Still haven't changed langue enuf, says the One.

Look what's comin, a port. Always a port, always a goddamned port.

These no-waves are like the previous none. Grey wi etchy white lines,
crackly lookin snippets, wavelengths or such. Port's a ghastly ghostly ville . . .

from here, 'll take a while. To get into. They'll wake up now, the ones.

Syntax says, peak of rose, peak of lily, one peaks of a structure
e'en a wave. Gibb'rish. Why speak Englush? Cause One knows it, that un . . .

This langue's fallin apart. Already, One? Words kin float around us

no-fish scales on the void. All the blessed. Pieces of chaos hum.
Not together, not tight but still stickin. Who are we? Not some parts . . .

Paris, 2010

About the Author

PHOTO BY DAVID BARNES

Alice Notley was born in Bisbee, Arizona, on November 8, 1945, and grew up mostly in Needles, California. She was educated in the Needles public schools, at Barnard College, and at the Writers' Workshop, University of Iowa. During the late sixties and early seventies, she lived a peripatetic, outlawish poet's life (San Francisco, Bolinas, London, Wivenhoe, Chicago) before settling on New York's Lower East Side. For sixteen years there, she was an important force in the eclectic second generation of the so-called New York School of poetry. In 1992 she moved to Paris and has lived there ever since, though retaining her ties to the United States, to New York, and to the desert. Notley has never tried to be anything but a poet, and all her ancillary activities have been directed to that end. She is the author of more than forty books of poetry. Her book-length epic poem *The Descent of Alette* was published by Penguin in 1996, followed by *Mysteries of Small Houses* (1998), which was one of three finalists for the Pulitzer Prize and also the winner of the *Los Angeles Times* Book Award for Poetry. More recent publications include *Grave of Light: New and Selected Poems 1970–2005,* for which she won the Academy of American Poets' Lenore Marshall Poetry Prize; *In the Pines*, which inspired an album of music by the indie duo AroarA; *Culture of One*, a verse novel set in a small desert town; the "everything book" *Benediction*; and *Eurynome's Sandals*, named for the goddess who danced the cosmos into existence. Notley has also received the Griffin Poetry Prize, the Shelley Memorial Award from the Poetry Society of America, an Academy Award in Literature from the American Academy of Arts and Letters, and the Poetry Foundation's Ruth Lilly Poetry Prize, which recognizes the outstanding lifetime achievement of a living US poet.